THE BASSET TABLE

broadview editi...
series edito

Portrait of Susanna Centlivre, by permission of the British Library.

THE BASSET TABLE

Susanna Centlivre

edited by Jane Milling

broadview editions

Library and Archives Canada Cataloguing in Publication

Centlivre, Susanna, 1667?-1723
     The basset table / Susanna Centlivre ; edited by Jane Milling.

(Broadview editions)
A play.
Includes bibliographical references.
ISBN 978-1-55111-678-5

     I. Milling, Jane, 1967- II. Title. III. Series: Broadview editions

PR3339.C6 B38 2009   822'.5   C2009-901293-6

Broadview Editions

The Broadview Editions series represents the ever-changing canon of literature by bringing together texts long regarded as classics with valuable lesser-known works.

Advisory editor for this volume: Michel Pharand

Broadview Press is an independent, international publishing house, incorporated in 1985. Broadview believes in shared ownership, both with its employees and with the general public; since the year 2000 Broadview shares have traded publicly on the Toronto Venture Exchange under the symbol BDP.

We welcome comments and suggestions regarding any aspect of our publications—please feel free to contact us at the addresses below or at broadview@broadviewpress.com.

North America
PO Box 1243, Peterborough, Ontario, Canada K9J 7H5
2215 Kenmore Ave., Buffalo, New York, USA 14207
Tel: (705) 743-8990; Fax: (705) 743-8353
email: customerservice@broadviewpress.com

UK, Ireland, and continental Europe
NBN International, Estover Road, Plymouth, UK PL6 7PY
Tel: 44 (0) 1752 202300; Fax: 44 (0) 1752 202330
email: enquiries@nbninternational.com

Australia and New Zealand
UNIREPS, University of New South Wales
Sydney, NSW, Australia 2052
Tel: 61 2 9385 0150; Fax: 61 2 9385 0155
email: info@unireps.com.au

www.broadviewpress.com

The interior of this book is printed on 100% recycled paper.

PRINTED IN CANADA

Contents

Acknowledgements

I would like to acknowledge the support of the library staff at the University of Cambridge, the Bodleian, the British Library, and the University of Exeter. For that daily support that makes life less of a gamble, thanks are due to Chris Smith.

Introduction

Susanna Centlivre and Writing for the Stage

Susanna Centlivre (1669-1723) was one of the most successful and significant dramatists of the eighteenth century. She was also one of the
most prolific, producing sixteen plays and three farcical afterpieces in
a writing career spanning 1700 to 1723. All except one of these plays, *A
Gotham Election* (1715), which was banned as too politically inflamma-
tory, were performed and all were published. Although Centlivre has
been less visible than her predecessor Aphra Behn in the twentieth-
and twenty-first-century theatrical repertoire, *The Gamester* (1705),
The Busie Body (1709), *The Wonder* (1714), and *A Bold Stroke for a Wife*
(1718) were standards of the eighteenth-century repertoire. Indeed,
Centlivre's name was also familiar to nineteenth-century audiences
because of the enduring popularity of her leading plays.

We have comparatively little biographical information about
Susanna Centlivre prior to her appearance in print in 1700. The
first account of her background appeared during her lifetime in
Giles Jacob's *The Poetical Register* (1719). Jacob set out to list the
major works and to provide some biography for the leading
playwrights of the day, authenticating his information as apparently from their own hands or from individuals who knew them.
In Jacob's politically inflected version of her life, Susanna was a
daughter of Parliamentarian Mr. Freeman of Holbeach, Lincoln-
shire. Her second marriage was to an army officer, Mr. Carroll,
under which name she wrote for the early part of her career, before
marrying Joseph Centlivre, Yeoman of the Mouth to Queen
Anne.[1] The second set of biographical information comes from
Abel Boyer's obituary in the December 1723 issue of his whiggish
journal *The Political State of Great Britain*. Boyer thought Centlivre's
maiden name was Rawkins and noted her marriage to "Carol,"

---

1   Joseph Centlivre was head chef and overseer of the Queen's kitchen. Giles Jacob, *The
    Poetical Register: or, The Lives and Characters of the English Dramatick Poets* (1719), 31-34.

followed by her marriage to Joseph Centlivre. However, he placed her lower on the social scale as coming from "mean Parentage, and Education."[1] Two later eighteenth-century biographers, John Mottley in *A Compleat List of All the English Dramatic Poets* (1747)[2] and William Chetwood in *The British Theatre: Containing the Lives of the English Dramatic Poets* (Dublin, 1750),[3] embellish the bare bones of her life story with more picaresque details such as a cruel stepmother, and have Centlivre running away to join a company of strolling players, and attending University dressed as a boy. These later, perhaps less reliable, accounts display the developments of eighteenth-century biography as a narrative and proto-fictional form, and yet there is evidence to support some of the more surprising details. Two overarching aspects emerge from these early biographies: first, the estimation of Centlivre as a major writer, and second, the party political character of her background, circle of acquaintance and her work, all of which reveal her sympathies with the Whig party.[4]

Centlivre's first foray into print, under her married name Carroll, was in a collection of letters gathered by Tom Brown, for Sam Briscoe, *Familiar and Courtly Letters* (1700). This publication connects Centlivre to a jobbing literary circle that included playwright George Farquhar[5] and critic John Dennis.[6] A second

---

1   Abel Boyer, *The Political State of Great Britain*, vol. 26 (1723), 670-71.

2   Mottley claims to have contributed two scenes to her play *A Bold Stroke for a Wife* (1718); "A Compleat List" was appended to Thomas Whincop's tragedy *Scanderbeg* (London: W. Reeve, 1747).

3   W.R. Chetwood was prompter at Drury Lane in 1722 or 1723 and may have known Centlivre through that theatre.

4   After the deposition of Catholic James II in 1688 and the "Glorious Revolution" that put Protestant William III in his place, Parliament had become increasingly powerful and political life had polarised into two political parties, the Whigs and the Tories. Broadly speaking the Tories stood for the preservation of the Anglican church from dissenters, the power of existing hierarchies such as the aristocracy, landed gentry, bishops etc., and the due succession of the monarchy. The Whigs were for a broad Protestant church, including dissenting religious belief, resistance to European Catholic expansion and the preservation of a Protestant monarchy, and acknowledgment of the place of those made wealthy through trade.

5   George Farquhar's (1676/7-1707) most successful play was *The Constant Couple* (1699), but he is best known today for *The Recruiting Officer* (1706) and *The Beaux' Stratagem* (1707).

6   John Dennis (1658-1734) was a literary critic and author of several plays.

book of letters, *Letters of Wit, Politicks and Morality* (1701), collected by Huguenot refugee Abel Boyer, places her work alongside Charles Gildon, Samuel Garth, William Burnaby, William Ayloffe, Richard Steele, Charles Johnson, and Jane Wiseman. All of these individuals wrote for the theatre and all demonstrated sympathy with the Whig party in their writing. As well as publishing Centlivre's correspondence, Boyer may have facilitated her first access to the stage. His play *Achilles* was produced at Drury Lane Theatre in the autumn of 1699, and in a letter of May 1700 he apologizes to Carroll that he has not yet managed to have her tragicomedy, *The Perjur'd Husband* (1700), staged.[1]

Centlivre was invited to contribute an elegy on John Dryden in a commemorative volume on the poet and playwright's death.[2] This linked her to a circle of writing women that included Lady Sarah Piers, Sarah Fyge Egerton, and three women playwrights: Delarivier Manley, Mary Pix, and Catharine Trotter. So it is clear that when Centlivre started writing for the theatre she was not a lone female entrepreneur. By the time she began her playwriting career in 1700, she could look to the examples of Katherine Philips, Aphra Behn, Trotter, Pix, and Manley. Of these, Behn was the best-known and most successful. Despite the political distance between the two writers (Behn had been a committed Tory), Centlivre considered it useful to borrow Behn's *nom-de-plume*, Astraea, in an early work, perhaps to mark herself as Behn's successor and to add weight to her entrance into the theatrical world.[3] Unlike other female dramatists of her day, who wrote in a wide range of genres, Centlivre made her living predominantly from the stage, only occasionally contributing political poems, prose essays, or letters to the burgeoning range of newspapers. Only Mary Pix was as committed to predominantly theatrical writing, whilst other writers such as Delarivier Manley and Eliza Haywood found

---

1   Abel Boyer, *Letters of Wit, Politicks and Morality* (1701), Letter XXXVIII, p. 359.

2   *The Nine Muses. Or, Poems Written by Nine several Ladies Upon the Death of the late Famous John Dryden, Esq.* (September 1700). This collection only just preceded the late September / early October production of Centlivre's *The Perjur'd Husband*. She complains in her preface that the play was produced before the season was in full swing, not a surprising decision for a new play from an unknown writer.

3   Abel Boyer, *Letters of Wit, Politicks and Morality* (1701).

prose, scandal writing, and novellas more attractive; and Catharine Trotter's theatrical work is less remembered now than her contribution to philosophical debates.

Centlivre's work was regularly performed, averaging around one play a season, an unprecedented output for any playwright in the first half of the eighteenth century, male or female. As early as 1702–03 she persuaded Lincoln's Inn Fields to take *The Stolen Heiress* in December, and the rival Drury Lane company to produce *Love's Contrivance* later in the season in June. Her work was primarily performed in London. Only once was she forced to travel to the new theatre at Bath with *Love at a Venture* (1706). Centlivre came to be regarded as a reliably bankable playwright by the theatre companies and was one of the very few writers for whom the stage provided a regular income. This is all the more surprising because over the course of the century "prejudice against women playwrights was fierce. They did get some work produced, but a startling number of the zero-compensation cases are plays by women."[1] It may have been the need to earn a living that accounts in part for Centlivre's prolific output. She certainly made few claims to poetic or literary status for her work, seemingly content to acknowledge that she wrote for bread.

Several of Centlivre's prefaces, prologues, and dedications indicate her frank interest in the financial side of writing for the stage.

> Writing is a kind of Lottery in this fickle Age, and Dependence on the Stage as precarious as the Cast of a Die; the Chance may turn up, and a Man may write to please the Town, but 'tis uncertain, since we see our best Authors sometimes fail.... I believe Mr. *Rich*[2] will own, he got more by the *Trip to the Jubilee*, with all its Irregularities than by the most uniform Piece the Stage cou'd boast of e'er since.[3]

One of Centlivre's early biographers, John Mottley, concentrates on her financial acumen and notes not only when her plays were successful in the theatre, but also the considerable sums and gifts that she earned from patrons for dedications and poems. Centlivre

---

1 Judith Milhous and Robert Hume, "Playwrights' Remuneration in Eighteenth-Century London," *Huntington Library Quarterly* 10.2–3 (1999), 44.

2 Christopher Rich (1647–1714) was patentee and manager of Drury Lane Theatre.

3 Preface, *Love's Contrivance* (London, 1703); see Appendix C2.

was able to find a socially significant and, almost without exception, whiggish dedicatee for the printed version of all but two of her plays. However, she indicates the limits of female economic power and of political patronage in a witty autobiographical poem, *A Woman's Case* (1721). Writing in the voice of her apparently disconsolate husband she complains:

> Why, 'faith, I think it very hard,
> So Brave a *Whig* is not prefer'd.
> One might have thought this Golden Age,
> You 'ad left off writing for the Stage;
> And from *South-Sea*[1] got Gold—true Sterling
> Enough to keep your coach, or Berlin.[2]

Because of her gender, Centlivre had not been advanced to a lucrative public post or place at court, despite her outspoken support for the succession of George I to the throne and even though the government was under the control of a Whig ministry guided by Robert Walpole.[3] Instead, in this poem she made an ingenious appeal to one of the South-Sea Company managers for a subscription to stock, since share-ownership was an enterprise that women were indeed able to pursue.[4] There is no evidence that she was granted the subscription, perhaps a blessing in disguise, since the South-Sea bubble was to burst the following year.

Part of Centlivre's theatrical success was due to her careful cultivation of the leading players of the day, as her prefaces, dedications,

---

1 The South-Sea Company, established in 1711, bought large swathes of government debt in return for interest from custom duties and the exclusive rights to trade with South American countries. Taking on the national debt in 1720, shares in the company were sold at increasingly inflated prices, making good returns for investors until the company debts so outstripped its income that the share price collapsed in 1722. Such frenzied stock and shareholding speculation was dubbed a "bubble" at the time.

2 *A Woman's Case* (London, 1720) and as "Letter from Mrs. C—e to Mr. Joy" in *A Miscellaneous Collection of Poems, Songs and Epigrams* (Dublin, 1721), 175-84.

3 Robert Walpole (1676-1745), Whig politician and the first *de facto* "prime minister" in 1721.

4 Susan Staves, "Investments, Votes and Bribes: Women as Shareholders in the Chartered National Companies," in Hilda Smith, ed., *Women Writers and the Early Modern British Political Tradition* (Cambridge: Cambridge UP, 1998), 259-78.

and other writings imply. Admittedly, the preface to her first play indicated some initial difficulties as she rather caustically suggested that "it only wanted the Addition of good Actors, and a full Town, to have brought me a sixth night."[1] However, by the time she was defending her adaptation of Molière's *Le Médecin Malgré Lui* as *Love's Contrivance*, she confessed herself:

> infinitely oblig'd to the Players, and in a great Measure the Success was owing to them, especially Mr. *Wilks*, who extended his Faculties to such a Pitch, that one may almost say he out-play'd himself ... I think my self extremely indebted to him, likewise to Mr. *Johnson*, who in his way I think the best Comedian of the Age.[2]

Centlivre was to discover the power of the performers to affect a performance run in the controversy that arose over *The Man's Bewitch'd* (1709). An article allegedly by Centlivre appeared in *The Female Tatler*, complaining about the actors' butchery of her script. The acting company withdrew the play from performance. In her preface to the play Centlivre admitted there had been problems with the company in rehearsal: the leading actor, Richard Estcourt had attempted to cut the ghost scene, and she suspected actor-manager Colley Cibber had kept it from running to the sixth night, and therefore her second benefit, by programming another play in its place. Although she defended the players—"I cou'd not have selected a better Company, nor had more Justice done to me in the Action"— she was piqued by their readiness to believe the *Female Tatler's* slur. Matters seem to have been quickly patched up, because by the time of *The Wonder* in 1714 Centlivre's preface extolled the close relationship between dramatist and actor:

> The Poet and the Player are like Soul and Body, indispensibly necessary to one another ... I freely acknowledge my self oblig'd to the

---

1 "To the Reader," *The Perjur'd Husband* (London, 1700). The only money a playwright made came from a "benefit," the income from ticket sales after house charges, on the third night of a play's run. If a play ran six nights consecutively the author would make a second benefit, and every third night thereafter as long as the play's initial run lasted.

2 Preface, *Love's Contrivance* (London, 1703); see Appendix C2.

Actors in general, and to Mr. *Wilks* and Mrs. *Oldfield*[1] in particular
... I must again repeat that which I meet with every where, I mean
the just Admiration of the Performance of Mr. *Wilks*, and Mrs.
Oldfield, and own that they much out-did in Action the strongest
of my Conceptions.[2]

It is also clear from all of Centlivre's dramatic writing that she
always had a weather eye on the performance of her work, and
frequently wrote parts for specific actors, particularly cultivating
Wilks and Oldfield, as *The Basset Table* reveals.

No playwright enjoys continued success in the theatre and the
ongoing repertoire without an ability to capture an audience.
Centlivre's writing had just those necessary qualities. Her forte was
comedy and farce, and her one tragedy, *The Cruel Gift* (1716), was
only averagely successful. From the start, her theatrical writing was
characterized by its carefully constructed plots and engaging dramatic action and contained a broad range of characters drawn from
all walks of life. She demonstrated a keen eye for theatrical effect
and self-reflexive performance moments and chose to treat topical
and important themes. Her plays have much lively action, where
lovers leap off balconies and conceal themselves in closets, under
tubs, and up chimneys. She created unusual action scenes, such
as the ghost scene that Estcourt felt so suspicious of in *The Man's
Bewitch'd* (1709) or the election riot of *A Gotham Election* (1715).
Her plays bustle with aspiring fops such as Ned Wou'dbe of *Love
at a Venture* (1706), country innocents such as Mrs. Dowdy of *The
Platonick Lady* (1706), or the doltish squire's son Num in *The Man's
Bewitch'd*, impudent servants, doting citizens, wrangling widows,
controlling fathers, and a vast array of vigorous young lovers.

As Centlivre's acquaintance with the theatre grew, she increasingly offered scenes that reflected on acting, performance, and the
playhouse itself. The use of disguise and of characters who act were
elements in many of her most successful plays, most notably *A Bold
Stroke for A Wife* (1718) where the hero Fainwell must adopt distinct
personalities to outwit Anne Lovely's four sets of guardians. This

---

1 Anne Oldfield (1683-1730) was a leading actress by this time and a friend of Centlivre's.
2 Preface, *The Wonder* (London, 1714).

mechanism reoccurs repeatedly in Centlivre's work; as Angelica disguises herself as a young spark to beat Valere at his own game of hazard and reform him in *The Gamester* (1705), and as Ensign Lovely disguises himself as the bluff Captain Match in *The Basset Table* (1705) to win Valeria from her father. Such muscular writing and plotting kept many of Centlivre's plays in repertoire throughout the eighteenth century. *The Basset Table* shares these elements, yet it is also anomalous as, uniquely in her work, we have no record of a revival after its first season. However, the themes it addresses, particularly its treatment of women and science, have rekindled interest for modern audiences and led to its regular performance in recent years.

The Basset Table and Performance History

The Basset Table is an example of Centlivre's financial and theatrical savvy. It is a companion piece to her very successful comedy *The Gamester* (February 1705), which was based on Jean-François Regnard's *Le Joueur* (1696). *The Gamester* had been Centlivre's first real theatrical success, running at Lincoln's Inn Fields for at least twelve nights and bringing her several benefits.[1] When the acting company headed by Thomas Betterton, Elizabeth Barry, and Ann Bracegirdle finally moved from Lincoln's Inn Fields to the new Haymarket Theatre in April 1705, prompter and early theatre historian, John Downes tells us that it was the play they chose to guarantee a respectable audience for their opening night of spoken drama.[2] After *The Gamester*'s success, and picking up many of the same concerns, *The Basset Table* added a new dimension with its central figure of the female gamester, Lady Reveller. It is not clear why Centlivre took this companion piece to the rival company at Drury Lane; however, the potential value of a follow-on to a suc-

---

1   Records of the repertoire of the two London theatres of this time are patchy. The fullest listing of theatrical events is recorded in W. van Lennep, E.L. Avery, et al., eds., *The London Stage 1660–1800* (Carbondale: Southern Illinois UP, 1960–68).

2   Judith Milhous and Robert Hume, eds, John Downes, *Roscius Anglicanus* (London: Society for Theatre Research, 1987), 100; the Haymarket's first offering of an Italian opera, *Gli Amori d'Ergasto*, in early April had not been a success.

cessful play would have been clear to both Centlivre and the players in the competitive theatrical market of 1705.[1] Trying to reproduce success in a sequel has always been a delicate and unreliable adventure. George Farquhar had tried with his *Sir Harry Wildair* (1701), an unashamed continuation of his smash hit of 1699, *The Constant Couple; or, A Trip to the Jubilee*, which had made Drury Lane a tidy profit, running for an astounding fifty-plus nights.[2] Robert Wilks had played the eponymous Sir Harry Wildair in both plays, and also took up the part of Sir James Courtly in *The Basset Table*. At several points in *The Basset Table*, in both stage directions and dialogue, Sir James Courtly is referred to as Sir Harry. We might view this as a printing or transcribing error, perhaps as evidence of the great speed with which Centlivre wrote her second gaming play in order to get it out early the following season, and we cannot know that the actors on stage would have actually chosen to articulate the "mistake." However, we might also read these slips as evidence of the intertextual connections of the stage; as a deliberate self-referential ploy to mark the kind of rakish character Sir James was to represent, and to ally *The Basset Table* not only to Centlivre's *The Gamester*, but also to the extremely lucrative *The Constant Couple*.

In the dedication of *The Basset Table* Centlivre paid lip service to convention and claimed she "endeavour'd to ridicule and Correct one of the most reigning Vices of the Age," but the play relishes the excitement of gambling culture. In particular, Centlivre created the attractive figure of Lady Reveller, a young, independently wealthy widow who earns considerable pin-money running a basset table—that is, hosting games of basset.[3] Lady Reveller shows little interest in changing her behaviour to please her suitor, the stolid Lord Worthy,

---

1 *The Basset Table* premièred at Drury Lane on 20 November, the night after Lincoln's Inn Fields had revived *The Gamester*.

2 See the Preface to *The Inconstant* (1702, n.p.), where Farquhar notes the play "brought the Play-house some fifty Audiences in five Months."

3 The rules of basset are fully explained in Appendix B1. In brief, players have thirteen cards laid out before them and place bets on whichever cards they choose. The dealer then turns up the first card, and any players with a bet on the same kind of card wins half their stake and the dealer / banker wins the other half. Players can defer their winnings on a card in order to multiply them by seven, then fifteen, thirty-three, or sixty-seven times. The dealer has a strategic financial advantage in the game.

until the rakish Sir James Courtly intervenes. In order to show her the error of her ways and aid his friend, Sir James lends her money at the table and then pretends to demand the return of his stake in the form of sexual favors to be taken by force. The conveniently placed Lord Worthy overhears and intervenes. The pretend rape attempt has a reforming effect on both parties. Although Lady Reveller remains eminently virtuous throughout the encounter, she appears to agree to forfeit the delights of the gambling table for the financial security that marriage to Lord Worthy can offer. Sir James's reputation is sullied by the pretend rape, particularly for the modern reader, and he too reforms and abjures gambling in order to be worthy enough to marry the ultra-virtuous Lady Lucy.

A second gambling plot, which centres on the potential threat to social hierarchy that gambling poses, is closely woven into this overarching structure. Mrs. Sago, a citizen's wife, embezzles her husband's stock in her obsessional determination to play at Lady Reveller's and mix with her betters, particularly Sir James Courtly. By the end of the play Mr. Sago faces ruin and the bailiffs, and threatens to separate from his gambling wife. However, he is too doting a husband and a reconciliation is achieved, with Mrs. Sago's extensive loses returned to Mr. Sago by Sir James, in a remarkable inversion of the circulating economy of gambling and trade. The play keys into the contemporary interest in gambling, social order, and gender, but does not offer the sentimental or simplistic moral images that were to occur in other gambling texts, such as Colley Cibber's *The Lady's Last Stake* (1708).

Meanwhile in a third plot, Sir Richard Plainman attempts to force his learned daughter Valeria into marriage with a bluff naval officer, Captain Hearty. Valeria's passion for natural philosophy, dissection, and experimentation is too much for the straightforward Hearty, and he colludes with her loyal suitor, the soldier Ensign Lovely, to bring about the young couple's marriage. Ensign Lovely has won Valeria's heart through his support for her scientific investigations, and disguised as the naval Captain Match, he wins her father's consent. The positive picture of Valeria's scientific aspiration and activity on stage was unique in the period and reflected the debate surrounding female education in Britain and France at the time.

Many elements of *The Basset Table* reveal Centlivre's alertness to performance and the strengths of the actors. Part of Lady Reveller's attraction to contemporary audiences would have been through the lively representation by Anne Oldfield. Oldfield had established herself in sprightly servant and second tier comic roles and her most successful part to date had been Lady Betty Modish in Cibber's *The Careless Husband* the previous season (1704). The pairing of Oldfield and Wilks as a sparring, romantic couple was to become a very successful formula and Centlivre's *Basset Table* was the first play to explore this stage chemistry in comedy.[1] Other actors for whom Centlivre created performance opportunities included a fine comic role for comedian and entrepreneur William Pinketh-man as Buckle, Lord Worthy's long-suffering servant. In Act III Buckle makes up a tragic story about his master's intended exile, which he performs as a glorious burlesque of heroic acting tradi-tions, throwing himself into the part with such gusto that Lady Reveller offers to have a word with the theatre managers to get him a job. Pinkethman had already had the opportunity to work the theatre audience in the prologue, where, in a novel innovation, he orchestrated audience participation by asking the gallery to clap him on cue, to demonstrate their power and his popularity.

The play employs some unusual stagecraft, beginning with a scene set below stairs, which uses the hirelings of the company to play servants waking up and racing after their employers following a late-night basset game.[2] Valeria's study full of scientific equipment, discovered in a reveal scene at the start of Act III, would have been a novel spectacle for audiences. This scene also added a new twist to the comic intrigue of concealing the lover, when poor Ensign Lovely is squashed under a tub that has just contained live fish. *The Basset Table* was one of the first plays to attempt to dramatize on stage the thrill and disappointments of the card table itself, devoting the whole of Act IV, scene ii to a basset game in full swing. Rather than setting the game in dumbshow, as in Thomas D'Urfey's *A Fool's Preferment* (1688), where downstage commentators Flea-flint

---

1 Wilks had been cast as the Duke of Norfolk and Oldfield as the ill-fated Mary Queen of Scots in *The Albion Queens* (1704), an adaptation of John Banks's *The Island Queens* (1684).

2 The scene echoes something of the opening to Thomas Southerne's *The Wives' Excuse* (1692), where gaming footmen await their masters from a music concert.

and Sharpe mock or interrogate the winners and losers as they depart from the table, Centlivre took the bold step of dramatising a game unfolding in all its emotional intensity. This followed the success of *The Gamester*, where in a similar scene the cross-dressed heroine Angelica is exposed to the full emotional cost of Valere's gambling at the dice game Hazard.

The Basset Table opened on 20 November 1705 and ran for four nights, garnering Centlivre one author's benefit.[1] Although we have no further contemporary performance records, the play was reprinted in 1706, which might suggest a second outing the following season. However, with the upheaval of that season when Richard Estcourt, William Pinkethman, and Susanna Mountfort remained at Drury Lane, while Wilks, Oldfield, and most other performers moved to the Queen's Theatre, it is possible that there was neither a taste for revival nor a financial incentive given the necessary rehearsals required to fill in the missing roles. The play languished commercially unstaged for over two centuries until interest in women's playwriting, and the play's themes, led to a series of revivals in the 1990s. The Company of Clerks, directed by Guy Retallack, staged a revival at the New End Theatre, London in August 1993, and Polly Irvin directed a collaboration between the Bristol Old Vic and the Tricycle Theatre, London, in 1998. Nancy Copeland briefly discusses these productions, both of which used a relatively brash, contemporary performance style, and led reviewers to debate Centlivre's feminist intentions in the play.[2]

Since then, the play has received numerous readings or performances in a university context, as the range of strong female roles and the play's interest in female scientific education have reintroduced it to university syllabi. The University of New Hampshire staged an adaptation as 1950s sitcom in 2000. Other college productions include Penn State School of Theatre (2000), City College, New York (2001),[3] Eastern Kentucky University

---

1 Avery, E.L., ed., *The London Stage, Part II 1700-1729* (Carbondale: Southern Illinois UP, 1968).

2 Nancy Copeland, *Staging Gender in Behn and Centlivre* (Aldershot: Ashgate, 2004), 165–66.

3 This production is discussed by director Kate Levin in *Restoration and Eighteenth-Century Theatre Research* 16 (2001), 97–111.

(2001), Juggernaut Theatre's reading in New York (2003), and Mountview Drama School, London (2004). The sudden interest in *The Basset Table* in recent years indicates the durability of Centlivre's stagecraft: the play remains eminently performable. Contemporary audiences have been captivated by several of the themes she tackles and by her creation of lively, independent female roles. The rest of this introduction looks in more detail at two significant themes: gambling and female education.

Gambling, the Stage, and Reform

Gambling was extremely popular with all sections of early eighteenth-century society. In writing two plays in 1705 that centre on gamesters, Centlivre was keying into both the popular taste for gaming and the very lively moral debate that had exploded around the topic. At the Restoration the Groom-Porter's apartments at court[1] had once again become a fashionable resort of the aristocracy, and high-stakes gambling, or deep play, became one of the markers of a libertine lifestyle and of aristocratic breeding for both men and women. Several recent critics have emphasized the function of gambling as performance; enobled by birthright, the aristocrat displayed at the gaming table his or her imperviousness to the power of money.[2] However, gambling was not restricted to the élite. Many inns in seventeenth- and eighteenth-century London were "ordinaries," which offered a meal for a fixed price followed by gaming. These drew the fashionable crowds and were also open to ordinary citizens, producing the potential for social mixing and the corruption of the social order that so vexed members of the reform societies. The evolution of gaming as a pursuit for the increasingly leisured gentry and the financially-successful

---

1   Since Tudor times the lucrative post of Groom-Porter had been responsible for arranging court gambling, supplying cards and dice, and resolving disputes.

2   Thomas Kavanagh, *Enlightenment and the Shadows of Chance: The Novel and the Culture of Gambling in Eighteenth-Century France* (Baltimore: Johns Hopkins UP, 1993); see also J. Evans, "'A Sceane of Uttmost Vanity': The Spectacle of Gambling in Late Stuart Culture," *Studies in Eighteenth-Century Culture*, 31 (2002), 1-20, and Beth Kowalski Wallace, "A Modest Defence of Gaming Women," *Studies in Eighteenth-Century Culture* 31 (2002), 21-40.

middling sort led to the development of summer entertainment locations outside London, such as Tunbridge Wells and Bath, where horseracing, gambling, and other fashionable pastimes were pursued. Books about gaming and instructions on playing were regularly published to capitalize on the new enthusiasm, notably Charles Cotton's *The Compleat Gamester* (see Appendix B1), which had six updated editions between 1674 and 1726, and was continued by Richard Seymour for five further editions through the eighteenth century. Pamphlets and stage plays depicted all social levels at play and celebrated the genteel gambler and the cunning of the rogue sharper, as in Theophilus Lucas's *Memoirs of the Lives, Intrigues, and Comical Adventures of the most Famous Gamesters* (London, 1714; see Appendix B4).

After the revolution of 1688 and the accession of William III to the throne, the celebratory rhetoric surrounding the Restoration court and its libertine excesses gave way to a more measured and moralistic tone. Gambling, though no less popular in fact in aristocratic circles or among the middling sort, began to be represented within a rhetoric of reform and was very rarely discussed without some framework of moral platitude and warning. So for the Marquis of Halifax writing "Advice to a Daughter" in 1704, deep, high-stakes play no longer represented a careless display of natural aristocratic worth, but raised pragmatic concerns about the circulation of money and financial loss.

To deep *Play* there will be yet greater *Objections*. It will give Occasion to the World to ask *spiteful Questions*. How you dare venture to *lose*, and what means you have to *pay* such great *sums*? If you pay *exactly*, it will be enquired from whence the *Money* cometh? If you owe, and especially to a Man, you must be so very *Civil* to him for his forbearance, that it layth a ground of having it farther improved, if the *Gentleman* is so disposed; who will be thought no unfair *Creditor*, if where the *Estate* faileth he seizeth upon the Person.[1]

---

1   George Savile, Marquis of Halifax, "Advice to a Daughter," *Miscellanies by the late Marquis of Halifax* (London, 1704), 82.

Here gambling no longer communicates an innate aristocratic value through social display, but has become a challenge to an interiorized value expressed as a moral and sexual code of behaviour, most particularly for the female gambler. Indeed, legislation from the Restoration onwards attempted to cap the potential losses incurred by any genteel gamester, and to limit the effectiveness of deep play as excessive display.

England's economic revolution in the late seventeenth century had seen the creation of a series of new financial mechanisms, including a greatly expanded stock-market and the establishment of the Bank of England. The economic revolution, driven in part by the need to fund William III's role in the exponentially expensive War of the Spanish Succession, offered a new context for understanding gambling as a form of financial risk-taking. The English state lottery was reintroduced in 1694 and, after a shaky start, became a more-or-less annual institution. Stock-jobbing and a nascent futures market had become the work of coffeehouses and "Exchange Alley."[1] Such economic speculation on shares was not always perceived as distinct from the activity of gamesters, as Defoe satirically commented, "Stock-jobbing is Play; a Box and Dice may be less dangerous, the Nature of them are alike, a Hazard ... are there fewer Sharpers and Setters in Exchange-Alley than at the Groom Porters?"[2] The battle for the legitimacy of the new financial mechanisms and the new financial class was frequently played out through the rhetoric of gambling. As Beth Kowalski Wallace suggests, "the attack on the illogic of the gambling table emerged simultaneously with an argument about the necessary logic behind the practices of nascent mercantile capitalism. In an attempt to argue for the 'rational' behavior of money under capitalism, reformers distinguish legitimate from illegitimate forms of risk and investment."[3] Gaming tended to be discussed in increasingly pejorative terms, and its evil consequences enumerated, in direct relation to the development of the speculative circulation of money within the new economy.

---

1   Jonathan's Coffee-House on Change Alley housed stockbrokers who were not allowed to trade at the Royal Exchange.

2   Daniel Defoe, *An Anatomy of Exchange Alley* (London, 1719), 43-4.

3   Beth Kowalski Wallace, "A Modest Defence of Gaming Women," *Studies in Eighteenth-Century Culture* 31 (2002), 26.

The potential for social upheaval offered by the new economic world exercised many, from the low-church Society for the Reformation of Manners to the non-juring[1] clergyman, Jeremy Collier. For these moral reformers, gambling produced a series of pernicious social ills: the mixing of social classes; the neglect of business when indulged in by the trading classes; the possible redistribution of wealth; the emotional disorder of the person and, for women in particular, sexual dissoluteness. Jeremy Collier, whose *A Short View of the Immorality and Profaneness of the English Stage* (1698) had caused a furore in the theatre world, weighed into the fray over gaming in his *Essay upon Gaming* (1713). This tract presented many of the reformers' arguments in the form of a comic dialogue between Dolomedes, the tricking gamester, and Callimachus, the voice of good manners and reason (see Appendix B3). Collier's overriding concern was for the maintenance of social distinctions between classes, as in so many of his works, and the potential ruin of trade that could result from excessive gaming. When Susanna Centlivre picked up on the contemporary interest and debate around gambling in *The Gamester* and *The Basset Table*, she echoed this reform rhetoric in the prefatory material to both. In her dedication to *The Basset Table*, Centlivre asserts:

> I have had a tender regard to good Manners, and by the main Drift of [this play], endeavour'd to ridicule and Correct one of the most reigning Vices of the Age.[2]

However, opinion was very much divided at the time of the play's performance as to whether *The Basset Table* either intended or managed to offer a reforming message.

For the social reformers of the day, Centlivre's play was certainly not a reformist work, as Anglican cleric Arthur Bedford's response illustrates (see Appendix D1). Indeed, the representational economy of the stage precluded any possibility of reform for many social reformers, who objected vociferously to the immorality of the stage at every opportunity. In response to those

---

1   A non-juror was someone who refused to swear an oath of allegiance to William III, opposing the usurpation of the established king James II.

2   Dedication, *The Basset Table* (London, 1706).

threatening the theatre, Centlivre discreetly adds her defence of the stage within the play itself, along very similar lines to theatre defenders such as John Dennis. She has her most censorious character, the virtuous and limited Lady Lucy, articulate the distinction between the dangers of the gaming table and the benefits of the stage:

LADY LUCY. I think the Play-house, the much more innocent and commendable Diversion.
LADY REVELLER. To be seen there every Night, in my Opinion, is more destructive to the Reputation.
LADY LUCY. Well, I had rather be noted every Night in the front Box, then, by my absence, once be suspected of Gaming; one ruins my Estate and Character, the other diverts my Temper, and improves my Mind. (54)

For Jeremy Collier, Arthur Bedford, and their ilk, there was no such nice distinction to be drawn between the two activities. The playhouse for them demonstrated all the ills of social interaction, unseemly display, profanity, and encouragement to sensual indulgence that the gaming table offered. Although Centlivre here contrasts the two spaces to the benefit of the stage, she does not condemn gambling outright. In *The Basset Table* the space of the gaming table and the function of gambling itself are ambivalently drawn.

For example, the dangers of social mixing that the reformers so bewailed are semi-mocked through cantankerous Sir Richard Plainman who upbraids Lady Reveller, "your Apartment is a Parade for Men of all Ranks, from the Duke to the Fidler" (51), with the concomitant implication of sexual access. Yet, neither Lady Reveller's status nor her reputation are threatened during the play. Moreover, Lady Reveller differs from the stage tradition of the avaricious female gamester: she is no Lady Trickitt who, in Southerne's *A Maid's Last Prayer* (1693), abdicates her class role and is depicted as greedily tallying up her bank at the end of an evening's basset, asserting "There's no true Friend, but Mony" (Act I, p. 8). Lady Reveller retains her social status, cynically dismissing both her citizen and male acquaintance; of Mrs. Sago she comments that "a Citizen's Wife is not to be endur'd amongst Quality; had she not Money, 'twere impossible to receive her" (65), and of Captain Hearty and Sir James she notes, "who cou'd endure these Men did they not lose their Money?" (103). Indeed, Lady Reveller's gaming seems to act as a marker of both her social status and her airy character, as a female counterfoil to Sir James Courtly.

The one character for whom there are consequences from the social mêlée of the basset table is Mrs. Sago, a citizen's wife. Mrs. Sago has used her access to commodities to wheedle money from her doting husband, in order to provide her with an entrée to the genteel world of Lady Reveller's basset table and to a liaison with Sir James Courtly. She ends the play firmly back in her city milieu at "Pin-makers Hall" (113), but this is the only consequence to her gaming and embezzlement. The disciplining of gambling among the lower sort was a stage trope that had been explored extensively since the late Restoration, and the Sago subplot to the play echoes Thomas D'Urfey's *A Fool's Preferment* (1688). In D'Urfey's play Cocklebrain, a country squire, is ruined by his wife Aurelia and her genteel gaming companions who, in order to keep him in town, dupe him into believing he has been elevated to a series of court posts. Rather than Aurelia, it is Cocklebrain who is punished, both for disinvesting in land and for believing that he might climb the social ladder to a dukedom. By contrast, in *The Basset Table* Mr. Sago's fortunes are saved at the last moment by an act of genteel generosity from Sir James Courtly, who returns the money he won from Mrs. Sago. "I believe you are the First Gamester that ever Refunded," Mr. Sago says (113). This unusual act demonstrates the careful distinction that Centlivre wished to draw for her audience between the amoral libertine aristocratic gamblers of earlier plays and the "airy" but good-mannered worth of Sir James Courtly. Courtly has identified himself as only a "middling Gentleman" in an exchange with Lady Lucy, quipping that "to Ruin Tradesmen is the Qualities Prerogative only; and none beneath a Lord can pretend to do't with an Honourable Air, ha, ha"(98). So, despite the reformist anxieties mouthed by Sir Richard Plainman and Lady Lucy, the social mixing of the basset table carries few consequences for Centlivre's characters.

A second great fear of the reformers was the disordering of the inner person that an obsession with gaming might induce; the loss of the proper, mannerly man or woman. Stage depictions of gaming were indeed traditionally used by playwrights to demonstrate the emotional range and humour of characters. One of the most popular tropes was the frenzy of the losing player, as depicted in Farquhar's *Sir Harry Wildair* (1701), where Lady Lurewell, Captain Fireball, and other losing gamesters race onto the stage in high dudgeon, tearing their cards and swearing. This is in marked contrast to the winner Sir Harry, whose insouciance indicates his status within the stage world and his function as disinterested aristocratic rake. Lady Lurewell is so emotionally disturbed by gambling that she promises Sir Harry sexual favours in return for further funds to play on. Such characters are in the mould of Wildblood in Dryden's *The Wild Gallant* (1663) or D'Urfey's *A Fool's Preferment* (1688), which offers a discovery scene of the basset table with "other Gentlemen and Ladies sitting round at Play ... several are standing by, and others walking about; Acting the several Humours of Winners and Losers" (Act II, scene i). Centlivre does create such a compulsive player in Valere in *The Gamester*, whose reclamation from the gaming table seems curiously provisional at the end of the play. By contrast, Lady Reveller in *The Basset Table* is far less emotionally disturbed by her gambling. This is in part because as the keeper of the basset table she is its regular beneficiary, and partly because she has been granted by Centlivre a version of that aristocratic disconnection from financial loss. In the game depicted in Act IV scene ii, Lady Reveller's engagement in play is no more frenzied than Sir James's and this distinguishes them from the lower-class Mrs. Sago and Captain Hearty, who are reduced to tears and fits of rage. When at the end of her resources at the table, in the heat of play, she ponders only "I never had such ill Luck,—I must fetch more Money" (102), before she discovers Sir James's apparently generous gift. When Sir James acts out his pretended rape scene, he accuses her:

> Can a Lady that loves Play so passionately as you do—that takes as much Pains to draw Men in to lose their Money, as a Town Miss to their Destruction—that Caresses all Sorts of People for your Interest, that divides your time between your Toylet and the *Basset-Table*; Can you, I say, boast of Innate Virtue? (106)

Yet his insistence on the clichéd correlation between the loss of virtue and play is more about the justification for his ruse to frighten her with a pretended rape, than any demonstration of her humour witnessed by the audience. Lady Reveller is no Aurelia, cuckolding and duping her husband in D'Urfey's *A Fool's Preferment*, nor is she the compulsive Lady Lurewell of Farquhar's *Sir Harry Wildair*.

Recent critical attention to Centlivre's *Basset Table* has centred on the figure of the female gamester and on the representation of gambling. Several critics have suggested that in her two gaming plays Centlivre was writing "reform" or "sentimental" comedy, but they find the alleged didactic message of both plays unsatisfying, offering "a highly competent if entirely implausible exercise in reform and reclamation."[1] A spate of recent criticism has re-examined the plays and questioned their generic designation as reform or sentimental, arguing instead that Centlivre was articulating the social anxieties of the economic shift from a landed to money-based economy.[2] For some critics, the reform of the female gamesters of *The Basset Table* is particularly ambivalent. Victoria Warren offers a feminist reading of Lady Reveller and Mrs. Sago, suggesting that audiences would have been disappointed by the loss of independence for these women once they reform and, thus, that their portrayal "reflects the countermovement of the text and helps to undercut the ostensible moral."[3] Beth Kowlaski Wallace finds Lady Reveller's early power as a widow quickly dissipated; she "is punished for her participation in one kind of rash and especially egregious economic display. As a widow who spends and circulates money as she wishes, Lady Reveller must be reined in and put under patriarchal control."[4] However, it is unclear quite how Lady Reveller is punished and Wallace also

---

1   Robert D. Hume, *The Development of English Drama in the Late Seventeenth Century* (Oxford: Clarendon, 1976), 469. James Evans in "A Sceane of Uttmost Spectacle" also argues the plays are "humane comedies" with a reform message.

2   LuAnn Venden Herrell, "Luck Be a Lady Tonight, or at Least Make Me a Gentleman: Economic Anxiety in Centlivre's *The Gamester*," *Studies in the Literary Imagination* 32. 2 (1999), 45–61.

3   Victoria Warren, "Gender and Genre in Susanna Centlivre's *The Gamester* and *The Basset Table*," *Studies in English Literature, 1500–1900* 43.3 (2003), 618.

4   Wallace, "A Modest Defence," 32.

suggests that through the powerful and attractive performance of the leading actresses, the apparently moral message of the play might be undercut.

Laura Rosenthal also looks at the paradox of the female gamblers in Centlivre's play, suggesting that Centlivre explores the limits of a "feminist individualism" through Lady Reveller, who retains self-ownership of her sexuality, relinquishing neither her virtue nor her reputation during Sir James's pretended rape. However, she concedes that Lady Reveller resists the paternal patriarchalism of Sir Richard, only to embrace the fraternal patriarchalism of Sir James and Lord Worthy, in agreeing to marriage and thus the transfer of her self-ownership and property to her husband.[1] Moreover, self-ownership is never permitted to the gambling wife figure, Mrs. Sago, who is bound by class, marital status, and learning within the sexual economy of patriarchy. Ultimately, Rosenthal concedes that, "in spite of Centlivre's feminist attempts to imagine some women as self-owners and consequently as owners of material and immaterial property, *The Basset Table* ultimately demonstrates the limits of Lockean individualism for feminists."[2] So, whilst most recent commentators are ambivalent about the feminist possibilities of the representation of female gamesters within the play, they agree that the play does not offer a reformist message, despite Centlivre's engagement with the reformers' rhetoric. The seductive compulsions of the basset table are depicted with theatrical delight, the gaming characters are by far the most performatively appealing of the play—indeed they are the plot's drivers—and the ills or consequences of gaming are so comically and lightly portrayed that it is difficult not to conclude with Arthur Bedford that, "before a Company of *Rakes*, *Spendthrifts*, and *Prodigals* (for such are most of those who resort to the *Play-Houses*) [the play] serves rather to sooth them in their *Vices*, and harden them in the contrary *Sin*."[3]

1   Laura Rosenthal, *Playwrights and Plagiarists in Early Modern England: Gender, Authorship and Literary Property* (Ithaca: Cornell UP, 1996), 237.

2   Rosenthal, *Playwrights and Plagiarists*, 241.

3   Arthur Bedford, *The Evil and Danger of Stage Plays* (Bristol, 1706), 127.

Women, Education, and Natural Philosophy

VALERIA: Dear, dear Philosophy, what immense pleasures dwell in thee! (70)

Despite its limited theatrical history, another key reason for the reawakened interest in *The Basset Table* is its portrayal of the learned lady. In Valeria, "a philosophical girl," Centlivre offered a sympathetic view of a young, female natural philosopher, a view that keyed into a lively contemporary debate on the education of women and the social function of natural philosophy. The discussion of women's place in society and more specifically the relationship between women and learning, the "querelle des femmes," had raged since the Renaissance, fuelled by works such as Christine de Pizan's *The Book of the City of Ladies* (1405) or Juan Luis Vives's *The Education of a Christian Woman* (1524). The late seventeenth century saw a return to heated debate across Europe. In France, this had been prompted by two factors—first, a secular one in the rise of an aristocratic, mixed-sex salon culture. Often presided over by leading women, salon culture was perceived as a politically inflected resistance to absolutism. Such a culture altered the visibility of educated women and produced female writers and thinkers who found Europe-wide popularity—for example Madeleine de Scudéry (1607-1701) and her politically astute scandal narratives. A second element in the debate about female education arose from religious roots, partly in response to this secular *précieuse* (learned lady) culture, through works such as François Fénelon's *Treatise on the Education of Girls* (1687), which argued for a religiously inflected, that is Catholic, education for young girls of the sort that Madame de Maintenon was developing at her religious school at Saint-Cyr.

In England, whilst there was no equivalent of the *précieuse* or salon culture, an increase in female literacy, the emergence of the middling sort as a social force, and the concomitant rise of print, broadened the call for more than aristocratic women to be educated. Bathsua Makin, who had tutored Charles I's daughter Elizabeth, issued *An Essay to Revive the Ancient Education of Gentlewomen* (1673), which acted in part as a prospectus for her school at Twickenham, and was inspired by Anna Maria Van

Schurman's *The Learned Maid: or, Whether a Maid may be a Scholar* (English translation, 1659). Judith Drake's *An Essay in Defence of the Female Sex* (1696) and Mary Astell's *A Serious Proposal to the Ladies* (1694; 1697) both used Tory Anglicanism to champion the capabilities of women and the religious benefits of their education.

In England the debate about the religious implications of female education was more fraught. Astell's *A Serious Proposal* called for a place of "*Religious Retirement*," where women would retreat from the world for educative purposes.[1] The idea of retirement to all-female institutions had a long heritage in writing on women and education, from Christine de Pizan's imaginings of a city for women, to Margaret Cavendish's *The Female Academy* in *Playes* (1662), which suggested a school-like environment for aristocratic women of wit and wisdom as a preparation for marriage. However, the French, Catholic implications of Astell's "Monastery" for women, whose model might be seen in the later development of the school at Saint-Cyr, caused a storm of satiric response from English writers. Defoe's *An Essay upon Projects* (1697) makes clear the limitations of a religiously-modelled education in his proposal:

> When I talk therefore of an Academy for Women, I mean both the Model, the Teaching, and the Government, different from what is propos'd by that Ingenious Lady, for whose Proposal I have a very great Esteem, and also a great Opinion of her Wit; different too from all sorts of Religious Confinement, and above all, from *Vows of Celibacy*. Wherefore the Academy I propose should differ but little from Publick Schools.[2]

In *The Basset Table*, the worldly Lady Reveller picks up this mockery in her quip to the philosophising Valeria, advising her to:

> bestow your Fortune in Founding a College for the Study of Philosophy, where none but Women should be admitted, and to Immortalize your Name, they should be called *Valerians*, ha, ha, ha.(65)

---

1   Mary Astell, *A Serious Proposal* (1694), 61.

2   Daniel Defoe, *An Essay upon Projects* (1697), 286-87, see Appendix A3.

To which the pert servant Alpiew adds that "All Men would not be excluded" given Valeria's love for Ensign Lovely. Essayists Joseph Addison and Richard Steele were still satirising the sexually-charged image of the nunnery implicit in the *Proposal* in the *Tatler* of 1709 (see Appendix A2).

Whilst writers from the Anglican tradition acknowledged that a spiritually-based education for women might produce benefits in the domestic and social realms, they were careful to distinguish such education from French and Catholic examples, often satirically. Likewise, the secular tradition of the *précieuse* did not escape ridicule. For example, the learned women in Molière's *Les Femmes Savantes* (1672) are given to fantastical rhetorical excess and are models of social and sexual disorder. When Thomas Wright adapted the play as *The Female Vertuoso's* (1693), he translated Molière's mockery of the *précieuse* into an English context, and set the learned women in relation to the learned men of the Royal Society of London. Lady Meanwell's interest in natural philosophy brings about the complete disintegration of the domestic order, because of the "Tryannical and Arbitrary Power of a Proud, Scolding, Whimsical, Philosophical Wife."[1] Although she has the trappings of natural philosophy, with a telescope on the roof and plans to open an "Academy of *Beaux Esprits* ... Woe then to the Royal Society," she is ridiculed by Sir Maggot Jingle as a mere projector (Act II, pp. 16, 23). Here the debate about women and education is translated into a debate about women and certain kinds of knowledge, in essence natural philosophy. However, despite the vitriol of Wright's play, it was by no means a given that women were excluded from the discourses of natural philosophy. Valeria in *The Basset Table* might have followed in the nascent stage tradition of the mocked virtuoso, particularly the female virtuoso, but her character offers a very different stage portrayal of the woman natural philosopher and reveals some of the economic, social, and gendered forces at work in the rise of natural philosophy itself.

The rise of natural philosophy in England was marked by the founding of the Royal Society in 1662, with its roots in the

---

1   Thomas Wright, *The Female Vertuoso's* (1693), Act V, p. 51.

European interchange of scientific ideas since the Renaissance and specifically in meetings of natural philosophers and amateur enthusiasts at Oxford during the 1640s. The upheavals of the Civil War and Commonwealth sharpened the Society's eagerness to pursue experimental activity and establish a mode of scientific enquiry and disagreement that distinguished itself from religious controversy, as Thomas Sprat, the Society's historian, emphasized.[1] Experimental practices developed through demonstrations for Society members and invited guests, and the dissemination of empirical data was established through experiments and the regular publication of findings. Such experimentation also had a political aspect, as John Henry summarizes:

> for Boyle and the other leading members of the Royal Society, solutions to the problems of knowledge were seen as solutions to the problem of how to establish and maintain order in the state. The reliable witnessing of experiments by gentlemen was the only sure way to establish matters of fact about the physical realm.[2]

The all-male membership of the Society included "professional" scientists such as Robert Hooke and Isaac Newton, aristocratic and genteel amateurs, as well as hybrid figures such as Robert Boyle. However, women were not excluded from the principles of experimentation and witnessing that underpinned the Society's activities, even though Margaret Cavendish seems to have been one of the very few female witnesses to visit the Society at Gresham College, Holborn.[3]

As well as demonstrations at Gresham College, the Society displayed and lectured in coffeehouses in order to broaden the exposure and appeal of experimentation and natural philosophy

---

1   Thomas Sprat, *History of the Royal Society* (1702), 55–56.

2   John Henry, *The Scientific Revolution and the Origins of Modern Science* (Basingstoke: Macmillan, 1997), 88. Robert Boyle (1627–1691) was an experimental scientist best known for his experiments with an air-pump.

3   Pepys's diary records that there was considerable debate about the probity of her invitation in 1667; see Samuel Pepys, *The Diary of Samuel Pepys*, ed. Robert Latham and William Matthews (Berkeley: U of California P, 1974), vol. 8, 243.

beyond the élite confines of Society membership.[1] Instrument makers were happy to supply versions of the natural philosophers' experimental equipment to any who could afford it, and often provided assistance in the use of instruments. Beyond the official publications of the Society in *Philosophical Transactions*, and the grand volumes such as Hooke's *Micrographia* (1665), the rise of print journals broadened the commentary and reporting on scientific advances. John Dunton's *Athenian Mercury* (1691-97) offered a small number of "experts" who answered questions from the middling sort predominantly on romantic and domestic matters, but some scientific and medical information and new discoveries were disseminated. The reach of such journals extended to the burgeoning provincial coffeehouses far beyond London, and clearly assumed both male and female readership.[2] The question-and-answer nature of the *Athenian Mercury* was echoed in several popularisations of science in dialogue form, most notably and popularly Bernard de Fontenelle's *Discourse on the Plurality of Worlds* (1686). Fontenelle became Secretary of the French Royal Academy of Sciences, but his dialogue between the natural philosopher and an aristocratic *précieuse* straddles the difference between scholastic and literary modes of writing.[3] He sets out in his preface the reason for casting one half of his dialogue as female:

> In this Discourse I have introduced a fair Lady to be Instructed in Philosophy, which, till now, never heard any speak of it; imagining by this Fiction I shall render my Work more agreeable, and to encourage the Fair Sex (who lose so much time at their Toylets in a less charming study) by the Example of a Lady who had no supernatural Character, and who never goes beyond the Bounds of a Person who has no Tincture of Learning, and yet understands all that is told to her.... And why should this Lady have Precedency over all the rest of her delicate Sex? Or do

---

1 Larry Stewart, *The Rise of Public Science* (Cambridge: Cambridge UP, 1992), 143-45.

2 Helen Berry, "An Early Coffee House Periodical and its Readers: the *Athenian Mercury*, 1691-1697," *The London Journal* 25.1 (2000), 14-33.

3 J.B. Shank, "Neither Natural Philosophy, Nor Science, Nor Literature," in Judith Zinsser, ed., *Men, Women and the Birthing of Modern Science* (DeKalb: Northern Illinois UP, 2005), 86-110.

they believe they are not as capable of conceiving that which she learned with so much Facility?[1]

Aphra Behn, in her Translator's Preface, considers his attempt to make natural philosophy comprehensible a failure, since he has mixed so much fantasy into the material that it is difficult to discern between what is "solid" and what is a "trifle." Moreover, she finds the Marquise figure unsatisfying: "he makes her say a great many silly Things, tho sometimes she makes Observations so learned, that the greatest Philosophers of Europe could make no better."[2] Nevertheless, a female interlocutor came to represent an attempt to reach a wider public in many later texts that set out to popularize mathematical or natural philosophic ideas, such as John Harris's *Astronomical Dialogues* (1719) or Francesco Algarotti's *Sir Isaac Newton's Philosophy Explain'd For the Use of the Ladies* (1737; translated by Elizabeth Carter 1739). This focus on the popularisation of natural philosophy did indeed unlock a rash of interest in experimental knowledge. Centlivre was certainly aware of this gendered representation of interest in science, and she apparently composed a complimentary poem for Anne Oldfield in the copy of Fontenelle's *Plurality of Worlds* she had borrowed from the actress.[3]

Valeria in *The Basset Table* is a remarkably positive image of the female natural philosopher, through whom Centlivre reworked the developing stage tradition of mockery of the virtuosi. Initially Royal Society members dubbed themselves *virtuosi*, appropriating a term for amateur enthusiasts and collectors, but by the 1700s the word had taken on more pejorative overtones as Gay, Fielding, and Pope's Dr. Fossile epitomized in *Three Hours after Marriage* (1717).[4] Valeria is not straightforwardly mocked as a virtuoso, but rather an equivocal picture emerges of her through

1   Bernard de Fontenelle, *A Discovery of New Worlds*, trans. Aphra Behn (London, 1688), "The Author's Preface," b2v.

2   Aphra Behn, "The Translator's Preface," Fontenelle, *A Discovery of New Worlds*, A8.

3   William Egerton, *Faithful Memoirs of the Life, Amours and Performances of … Mrs. Anne Oldfield* (London, 1731), 58.

4   Dr. Fossile is depicted as a pedantic collector of scientific curiosities, and obsessed with useless and arcane knowledge.

three means: the comments other characters make about her, her philosophical language, and her scientific equipment and activity. Valeria is undoubtedly designed as a comic character; she is dubbed a "she-philosopher" and both her philosophic language and mode of discourse are commented on negatively by other characters. Ensign Lovely, her admirer, reports that she has claimed "that fire cannot burn, nor Water Drown, nor Pain Afflict and forty ridiculous Systems" (56), and Lady Reveller complains "she'll prove by and by out of *Discartes*, that we are all Machines"(67). Both attitudes seem self-evidently contradictory or erroneous. However, they are in fact gentle exaggerations of the growing mechanical philosophy indeed championed by René Descartes, but modified by recent experimental investigations. Ensign Lovely also ridicules Valeria's attention to reptiles and insects, by this point something of a cliché derived from the early natural philosophers' interest in these creatures, and Centlivre does offer the audience a shorthand image of Valeria's interests by first introducing her running on stage in hot pursuit of a "huge flesh fly." More significantly, Valeria is criticized because of her mode of philosophising—she will not brook contradiction. Despite their negative connotations, however, all of these aspects in fact establish Valeria's credentials as a true natural philosopher and virtuoso.

Secondly, we might consider the representation of her scientific equipment. The stage tradition tends to the ridicule of such instruments, as in Behn's commedia-based farce *The Emperor of the Moon* (1687), where the Doctor enters "with all Manner of Mathematical Instruments hanging at his girdle; Scaramouch bearing a Telescope twenty (or more) Foot long."[1] The reveal scene of Valeria in her study is reminiscent of Sir Nicholas Gimcrack in Shadwell's *The Virtuoso*. However, Sir Nicholas is far more ridiculed; for example, he is discovered learning to swim on his study table (Act II, scene ii). Nor does Shadwell's play call for the legitimating range of books and instruments that Centlivre wants in order to set the scene for Valeria:

---

1   Aphra Behn, *The Emperor of the Moon* (1687), p. 7.

The Scene draws, and discovers Valeria with Books upon a Table, a Microscope, putting a Fish upon it, several Animals lying by. (000)

Some of the equipment in Valeria's study, notably the microscope, would still have been rare and expensive objects in their day. Pepys paid five pounds ten shillings for his microscope, which came with prepared slides.[1] In *The Virtuoso*, Clarinda thinks her uncle, Sir Nicholas

> a sot that has spent two thousand pounds in microscopes to find out the nature of eels in vinegar, mites in a cheese, and the blue of plums which he has subtly found out to be living creatures. (Act I, scene ii)

This might well be something of an overstatement, to prove Gimcrack's profligate spending, which eventually ruins his estate. After all, even the foremost optical instrument maker of the Restoration period, Richard Reeve's sixty-foot telescope was valued at a mere 100 pounds.[2] Later in the eighteenth century cheaper, pocket telescopes and small-scale microscopes were more readily available for the amateur enthusiast, male and female. We have no information about the kind of stage prop the theatre used for Valeria. However, it needed to be both immediately recognisable as a microscope and clearly visible to the audience. Given that this is a discovery scene and thus the table is situated behind the first set of shutters,[3] it might seem sensible to suggest that the prop looked similar to Hooke's microscope, illustrated so famously in his *Micrographia* (1665), which would be both of an appropriately visible size and an iconic image of scientific enquiry. In essence Centlivre is asking the theatre to recreate for Valeria the markers of the legitimate study of a "professional" scientist, rather than mock-

---

1   Lisa Jardine, *Ingenious Pursuits: Building the Scientific Revolution* (London: Little and Brown, 1999), 43.

2   Jardine, *Ingenious Pursuits*, 47.

3   Scene changes on the Restoration stage were effected by moving pairs of painted shutters together. Most performance occurred on the well-lit (by candles) forestage, with the shutters acting as a painted backdrop.

ing the aspiration of a virtuoso through exaggerated equipment.

Finally, Valeria's use of the microscope as a stage prop raises interesting questions about the relationship between the public demonstrations of scientific experiments at the Royal Society and the staging of experiments on stage. The use of instruments itself marks the rise of the experimental ethos in natural philosophy, and here the stage acts as a secondary, doubled forum of display in the authentication of experimental science. Valeria's experimentation is an example of good scientific method: she uses a microscope to look at blood circulating in live fish that she keeps ready in a tub nearby. In this and in her interest in tapeworms, she accurately parrots the work of Edward Tyson, a comparative anatomist and member of the Royal Society.[1] In dissecting a dove in the search for gall, she may be following Anthony van Leeuwenhoek, who published his findings on gall in trout in *Philosophical Transactions*.[2]

The parody in this experimentation scene is very subtle, with the parodic element lying only in the "inappropriate" image of the female figure in place of the natural philosopher. Valeria is in many ways celebrated by Centlivre's play as a model of an experimental scientist, whose activity is not disciplined by the play, since it does not disrupt her marriage to the appropriate suitor, Ensign Lovely. Valeria is not required to foreswear her experimentation after marriage, nor is it presented as a bar to domestic order, in marked contrast to the projecting, sexually deviant, disorderly female *virtuosi* of Thomas Wright's play. It is this positive figure of the independent, learned female, who marks herself as one of the "rational creatures" of the play, that has in part accounted for the play's return to university syllabi and to the stage.

---

1 Tyson published several papers on dissecting tapeworms in the Royal Society's *Philosophical Transactions* in 1683 and 1691.

2 Anthony van Leeuwenhoek, "An Extract of a Letter from Mr. Anthony Van Leeuwenhoek, to the R.S. Containing His Observations ... On the Skin of the Hand, and Pores, of Sweat, the Crystalline Humour, Optic Nerues, Gall, and Scales of Fishes," *Philosophical Transactions (1683-1775)*, vol. 17 (1693), 949-60.

Susanna Centlivre: A Brief Chronology

c. 1670	Born, probably Susanna Freeman, probably near Holbeach, Lincolnshire.
1688	William III and Mary ascend to throne vacated by James II in "Glorious Revolution."
before 1700	Susanna marries or has liaison with "nephew of Sir Stephen Fox," possibly Mr. Rawkins, who dies shortly afterwards; marries an army officer called Carroll, who was apparently killed in a duel. Writes under the name Carroll for early years of her career.
1700	Resident in London. Publishes letters in Sam Briscoe's *Familiar and Courtly Letters* (edited by Tom Brown, London) and elegy as "Polimnia" in *The Nine Muses*, a collection of poems by women on the death of John Dryden. First play, a tragi-comedy, *The Perjur'd Husband: or, The Adventures of Venice*, performed Drury Lane, September or October (published London, 1700).
1701	Publishes letters in Abel Boyer's *Letters of Wit, Politicks and Morality* (London), and in Sam Briscoe's *Familiar and Courtly Letters*, volume II.
1702	William III dies, succeeded by Queen Anne. *The Beau's Duel: or, A Soldier for the Ladies* performed Lincoln's Inn Fields, in June (London, 1702). *The Stolen Heiress: or, The Salamanca Doctor Outplotted* performed the following season at Lincoln's Inn Fields, in December (London, 1703).
1703	*Love's Contrivance: or, Le Médecin Malgré Lui* performed at Drury Lane in June (London, 1703).
1705	*The Gamester* performed Lincoln's Inn Fields around February (London, 1705). *The Basset Table* performed the following season at Drury Lane (London, 1706).
1706	*Love at a Venture* performed by the Duke of Grafton's Servants at the New Theatre, Bath (London, 1706).

The Platonick Lady performed Haymarket, November (London, 1707).

1707   23 April Susanna marries Joseph Centlivre, Yeoman of the Mouth to Queen Anne.

1709   *The Busie Body* performed Drury Lane in May (London, 1709).

The Man's Bewitch'd: or, The Devil to Do about Her performed the following season at Haymarket, December (London, 1709).

1710   Short farce *A Bickerstaff's Burying: or, Work for the Upholders* performed Drury Lane, March (London, 1710).

Mar-plot, or, The Second Part of the Busie-Body performed the following season at Drury Lane in December (London, 1711).

1712   *The Perplex'd Lovers* performed Drury Lane in January (London, 1712).

Takes up residence in Buckingham Court, Charing Cross, London.

1713   Poems including "The Masquerade. A Poem. Humbly Inscribed to his Grace the Duke D'Aumont."

1714   *The Wonder: or, A Woman Keeps a Secret* performed Drury Lane in April (London, 1714).

Poem "On the Right Hon. Charles Earl of Halifax being made Knight of the Garter."

Queen Anne dies, succeeded by George I, Elector of Hanover.

1715   Poems to royalty and Whig dignitaries "An Epistle to Mrs. Wallup, Now in the Train of Her Royal Highness, the Princess of Wales"; "A Poem. Humbly Presented to His most Sacred Majesty George, King of Great Britain, France and Ireland. Upon his Accession to the Throne"; "To her Royal Highness the Princess of Wales at her Toylet, on New-Year's Day."

Short satirical farce on electioneering, *A Gotham Election*, banned 1715 (London, 1715).

Short farce *A Wife Well Manag'd* (London, 1715) eventually performed at the New Theatre over against the Opera House, Haymarket, March 1724.

1716	*The Cruel Gift: or, The Royal Resentment*, Centlivre's only tragedy, performed Drury Lane in December (London, 1717).
	Poems published in Whig collections or journals: "Ode to Hygeia" on Robert Walpole; "Upon the Bells ringing at St. Martin's in the Fields, on St. George's Day, 1716, being the Anniversary of Queen Anne's Coronation"; "The Patriots"; "These Verses were writ on King George's Birthday."
	Supposed to have a hand in *The Catholic Poet*, an attack on Alexander Pope, hence Pope's response in *The Dunciad*.
1717	Poem "An Epistle to the King of Sweden from a Lady of Great-Britain."
1718	*A Bold Stroke for a Wife* performed at Lincoln's Inn Fields in February (London, 1718).
	Poem "From the Country to Mr. Rowe in Town. M.DCC.XVIII."
1719	Poem published "A Pastoral to the Honoured Memory of Mr. Rowe."
1720	Poems published: "To the Duchess of Bolton, Upon seeing her Picture drawn unlike her"; "To the Earl of Warwick, On his Birthday"; the autobiographical "A Woman's Case: in an Epistle to Charles Joye, Esq. Deputy-Governor of the South Sea."
	Anti-Jacobite and anti-Catholic articles in the whiggish *Weekly Journal*, September and October.
1722	Poem published celebrating the anniversary of George I's coronation.
	The Artifice performed at Drury Lane in October (London, 1723).
1723	Susanna Centlivre dies on 1 December, and is buried in St. Paul's Church, Covent Garden.

A Note on the Text

This edition is based on the first edition of the play printed for William Turner and J. Nutt in 1705, despite the 1706 date on the text, very shortly after the performance of *The Basset Table* at Drury Lane. The copy-text is Narcissus Luttrell's copy, dated 4 December 1705, from the Bodleian Library (Q1). I have collated this text against the Cambridge University copy (Q2) and the Yale quarto first edition reproduced in Richard Frushell's *The Plays of Susanna Centlivre* (Q3). The duodecimo second edition printed for Jonas Browne and S. Chapman in 1706 (D1) makes some corrections of spelling and one or two substantive alterations to the text, which I have incorporated for ease of reading. Some textual clarifications were attempted by the third edition, printed in 1735. Textual variations are recorded in the textual notes and indicated in the text with the symbol †.

Jacqueline Pearson's useful article, "Textual Variants and Inconsistencies in Susanna Centlivre's *The Basset-Table* (1705)," in *Restoration and Eighteenth-Century Theatre Research* 15.2 (2000), 40-59, identifies some of the flaws of the first edition. However, in the text that follows I have taken a light touch, offering little editorial alteration. I have preserved most of the first edition punctuation, unless it makes the sense unclear, and retained most of the spelling; thus, for example, "cannot" is shortened to "cann't" in this text rather than the more familiar "can't". All stage directions are from the first edition and have only been moved where their original placement on the page, due to space constraints in printing the first edition, made them unclear. The presentation of stage directions has been standardized and speech prefixes have been expanded and corrected from the first edition, for clarity.

Something that the reader will immediately notice in the text is Centlivre's prolific use of the long dash. The length of the dashes in this edition has been standardized, since in the first edition the printers produced dashes of different lengths, but only in relation to the space of the printed line, not as an indication of different kinds of ellipsis or distinct punctuation. The use of dashes gives the impression of speed in speech, and has led some commentators to suggest that Centlivre herself was composing quickly and did not take time to correct her text. However, the dash is a mechanism that she uses throughout most of her comedic work, although it is most marked in her two comedies of 1705, *The Gamester* and *The Basset Table*. In this play the dashes serve a variety of different functions: to mark a change of addressee, including occasionally marking an aside; to mark a change of thought or tone; to indicate that the speech is interrupted; to imply emotional distress and indicate a disrupted breathing pattern for the performer; to imply confusion or hesitation, that is to support the actor's interpretation of the role; to indicate acted or mimicked speech; or to indicate action. Overall, the use of the dash indicates Centlivre's keen sense of writing for performance, rather than for the reader.

THE

BASSET-Table.

A

COMEDY.

As it is Acted at the *Theatre-Royal* in *Drury-Lane*, by Her Majesty's Servants.

By the Author of the Gamester.

L O N D O N:

Printed for *William Turner* at the *Angel* at *Lincolns-Inn-Back-Gate* ; and Sold by *J. Nutt* near *Stationers-Hall,* 1706. Price 1 *s.* 6 *d.*

Title page, *The Basset Table*, by permission of The Bodleian Library, University of Oxford.

Illustration of the basset players from Act IV, by permission of the British Library.

THE BASSET-TABLE

A COMEDY

As it is Acted at the *Theatre-Royal* in *Drury-Lane,* by Her
Majesty's Servants.
By the Author of the Gamester.

London: Printed for *William Turner* at the *Angel* at *Lincolns-Inn-
Back-Gate*; and Sold by *J.Nutt* near *Stationers-Hall,* 1706.
Price 1s. 6d.

TO THE RIGHT HONOURABLE
ARTHUR
LORD *ALTHAM,*
BARON OF *ALTHAM,*
IN THE KINGDOM OF IRELAND.

My LORD,

Poetry, in its first Institution, was principally design'd to Correct, and rectify Manners. Thence it was that the *Roman* and *Athenian Stages* were accounted Schools of Divinity and Morality; where the Tragick Writers of those Days inspired their Audiences with *Noble* and *Heroick Sentiments,* and the *Comick* laugh'd and diverted them out of their *Vices*; and by ridiculing *Folly, Intemperance,*†[1] and *Debauchery,* gave them an Indignation for those Irregularities, and made them pursue the opposite *Virtues.*

This caus'd the *Dramatic Poets,* in ancient Times, not only to be reverenc'd by the lower sort of People, but highly Esteem'd and Courted by Persons of the first Rank; and tho' the Writers of latter Ages, have, in a greater Measure, not to say in a scandalous† Manner, deviated from the Foot-steps, and Examples of their Predecessors; yet have they found Protection and Favour with those, who have been so Generous as to ascribe the Faults of the *Poets* to the Degeneracy of the *Age* wherein they liv'd.

This consideration, *my Lord,* has imbolden'd me to this Address, for tho' on the one Hand I am sensible, that the following Piece does little Merit your *Lordship's* Patronage; yet your innate Goodness and Generosity give me hopes, that your Lordship will Pardon this Intrusion, in which I have the Examples of all those that *wrote* before me to bear me out. I heartily wish this Play were more worthy of your *Lordship's* Acceptance: Yet so much, I hope, will be forgiven to the fondness of a Mother for her Production; if, I say, in its Favour, that through the whole Piece, I have had a tender regard to good Manners, and by the main Drift of it,

---

1   † indicates a textual variation; see below, p. 117.

endeavour'd to ridicule† and Correct one of the most reigning Vices of the Age. I might say, as many of my *Brethren* have done upon slighter Grounds, that this Play has had the good Fortune to Please and Divert the Nicest, and Politest Part of the Town; but I should set little Stress on their Applause, had I not some reason to depend upon your *Lordship's* Approbation, whose Judgement, Penetration and Discernment, are alone sufficient to do full Justice to a performance of this Kind.

And now, my *Lord*, if I follow'd the beaten Road of Dedicators, it would naturally Engage me in a *Panegirick*, upon your Lordship's Personal Virtues, and those of your *Noble* and *Pious Family*; but I shall purposely decline a Talk to which I freely own my Ability is Unequal, and which, tho' manag'd by a *Masterly Pen*, would make your Modesty suffer. Therefore I shall conclude, with begging your *Lordship*'s leave to Subscribe my self, with all imaginable Respect and Sincerity.

My LORD,

Your Lordship's most Obedient,

and most Devoted

Humble Servant,

PROLOGUE

Spoke by Mr. Penkethman.[1]

In all the Faces that to Plays Resort,
Whether of Country, City, Mob or Court;
I've always found that none such hopes Inspire,
As you—dear Brethren of the Upper Tire.[2]
Poets, in Prologues,† may both Preach and Rail,
Yet all their Wisdom, nothing will avail,
Who writes not up to you, 'tis ten to one will fail.
Your thundring plaudit 'tis that deals out Fame,
You make Plays run, tho' of themselves but Lame:
How often have we known your Noise Commanding,
Impose on your Inferior Masters Understanding;[3]
Therefore, Dear Brethren, (since I am one of you)
Whether adorn'd in Grey, Green, Brown or Blue,
This day stand all by me, as I will fall by you,
And now to let—
The poor Pit see how Pinky's Voice Commands,
Silence—Now rattle all your Sticks, and clap your grimy Hands.
I greet your Love—and let the vainest Author show,
Half this Command on clearer Hands below,
Nay, more to prove your Interest, let this Play live by you.
So may you share good Claret with your Masters,
Still free in your Amours from their Disasters;
Free from poor House-keeping, where Peck[4] is under Locks.
Free from Cold Kitchings, and no Christmas Box:

---

1 William Pinkethman, or Pinky, (d. 1725) was a well-known theatrical entrepreneur
   and low comedian.

2 The upper tier or gallery, containing the cheapest seats in the house, was known as the
   preserve of the servant class.

3 The gentry and well-to-do tended to sit in the pit or boxes of the first gallery.

4 Slang for meat or food. Nathan Bailey's *The New Universal English Dictionary... to which
   is added, a dictionary of cant words* (London, 1759).

So may no long Debates i'th'House of Commons,
Make you in the Lobby Starve, when hunger† Summons;
But may your plenteous† Vails¹ come flowing in,
Give you a lucky hit, and make you Gentlemen;
And thus preferr'd, ne'er fear the World's Reproaches,
But shake your Elbows with my Lord, and keep your Coaches:

---

1   Tips given to a servant. The OED suggests that servants were largely paid by such gratuities.

EPILOGUE

Spoke by Mr. Esthcourt.

This goodly Fabrick to a gazing Tarr,
Seems Fore and Aft, a Three Deckt-man of War.
Abast, the Hold's the Pit, from thence look up,
Aloft! that Swabber's Nest, that's the Main-Top.[1]
Side-boxes mann'd with Beau, and modish Rake,
Are like the Fore-castle, and Quarter-Deck.[2]
Those dark disguised, advent'rous, black-nos'd[3] *few,*
May pass for Gunners, or a Fire-ship's Crew.
Some come like Privateers a Prize to seize,
And catch the French *within the Narrow Seas.*
The Orange-Ladies, Virgins of Renown,
Are Powder-Monkies[4] *running up and down.*
We've here our Calms, our Storms, and prosp'rous Gales,
And shift our Scenes as Seamen shift their Sails.
The Ship's well mann'd, and not ill Woman'd neither,
So Ballast'd and Stow'd, my Lads, she'll bear the Weather.
But greater Dangers vent'ring† Players alarm,
This Night's Engagement's worse than any Storm.
The Poet's Captain, but half dead with fright,
She leaves her Officers to maintain the Fight;
Yond middle Teer with Eighteen Pounders maul us,†
That Upper-Deck with Great and Small-Shot gauls us.
But from this Lower-Teer most Harm befals,

---

1   In the metaphor of the epilogue, the upper gallery becomes the maintop, a platform
    on the mainmast, occupied by lowly sailors, who swabbed the deck.

2   The forecastle, the raised front deck of a ship and the quarter-deck, a small deck
    between the stern and the mast, were the preserve of the officers on board.

3   Black patches were frequently worn on the nose to disguise venereal disease. Women
    sometimes wore black masks to attend the theatre, although they might be suspected
    of being prostitutes if they did so.

4   Powder-monkeys were usually boys on ship, who kept the gunners supplied with
    gunpowder.

There's no opposing their prevailing Balls.
As either Foe or Friend their Chain-shot[1] flies,
We sink or swim, we Conquer, Fall or Rise.
To fit and rig our Ships much Pains we take;
Grant we may now a Saving-Voyage make.
Here we're Embark'd, and as you Smile or Frown,
You are our Stars, by You we Live or Drown.

---

1   "Two balls, or half-balls, connected by a chain" (*OED*).

DRAMATIS PERSONAE

MEN

Mr. Mills,—*Lord* Worthy—*In Love with Lady* Reveller, *a hater of Gaming.*

Mr. Wilks,—*Sir* James Courtly—*An airy Gentleman, given to Gaming.*

Mr. Bigerstaff,[1]—Lovely *an Ensign*—*In Love with* Valeria.

Mr. Bullock,—*Sir* Rich. Plainman—*Formerly a Citizen, but now lives in* Covent-Garden, *a great lover of a Soldier, and an Inveterate† Enemy to the* French.

Mr. Esthcourt,—*Captain* Hearty—*A Sea Officer, design'd by Sir* Richard *to Marry* Valeria.

Mr. Johnson,—Sago—*A* Drugster *in the City, very fond of his Wife.*

Mr. Penkethman,—Buckle—*Footman to Lord* Worthy.

WOMEN.

Mrs. Oldfield,—*Lady* Reveller—*A Coquetish Widow, that keeps a* Basset-Table.

Mrs. Rogers,—*Lady* Lucy—*Her Cousin, a Religious sober Lady.*

Mrs. Montford,[2]—Valeria—*A Philosophical Girl, Daughter to Sir* Richard, *in Love with* Lovely.

Mrs. Cross,—*Mrs.* Sago†—*The* Drugster's *Wife, a Gaming profuse Woman, great with my Lady* Reveller, *in Love with Sir* James.

Mrs. Lucas,—*Alpiew*[3]—*Woman to Lady* Reveller.

---

1 John Bickerstaff (fl. 1703-24).

2 Susanna Mountfort (1690-1720); daughter of William Mountfort and Susanna Mountfort Verbruggen, this was young Susanna's first full theatrical season at Drury Lane.

3 Alpiew is a term from basset meaning to turn up the corner of a winning card in order to bet on it again and double your winnings.

Ladies, Gentlemen, for the Basset-Table.
Chair-man, Foot-men, &c.

Scene. *Lady* Reveller's *Lodgings in* Covent-Garden; *the Time, Four of the Clock in the Morning.*

THE BASSET TABLE

ACT I

A large Hall, a Porter with a Staff, several Chairs Waiting, and Footmen a-sleep, with Torches and Flambeauxs standing about the Room.

FOOTMAN. Certainly they'l Play all Night, this is a cursed Life.

PORTER. How long have you liv'd with your Lady?

FOOTMAN. A Month, too long by thirty Days, if this be her way of living; I shall be dead before the Year's out; she Games all Night, and Sleeps all Day.

PORTER. As long as you sleep, what's Matter?

FOOTMAN. But I do not, for while she sleeps, I'm Employ'd in Howdee's, from one end of the Town to the other.

PORTER. But you rest while she's Gaming; What would you do, if you led my Life? This is my Lady's constant Practice.

FOOTMAN. Your Lady keeps a *Basset Table*, much good may it do you with your Service—Hark, they are broke up. (*Within.*) Ha, hy, my Lady *Gamewel*'s Chair ready there—Mr. *Sonica*'s Servant.[1] (*The Footmen wake in a hurry.*)

FIRST FOOTMAN. Where the Devil is my Flambeaux?

SECOND FOOTMAN. So-hey—*Robin*, get the Chair ready, my Lady's coming; stay, stay, let me light my Flambeaux.

THIRD FOOTMAN. (*Waking.*) Hey, hoa, what han't they done Play yet?

PORTER. They are now coming down, but your Lady is gone half an hour ago.

THIRD FOOTMAN. The Devil she is, why did you not call me?

PORTER. I did not see you.

---

1 Sonica is the name in basset given to a card which arrives early and causes a player to win or lose, so the word came to mean immediately, at once. From Thomas Dyche, *Nouveau Dictionnaire Universel* (Avignon, 1756), II, 418.

THIRD FOOTMAN. Was you Blind?—She has lost her Money, that's certain—She never flinches upon a Winning-Hand—her Plate and Jewels Walks to Morrow to replenish her Pocket—a Pox of Gaming, I say. (*Exit.*)

(*Within.*) Mr. *Looseall's* Man—

FOURTH FOOTMAN. Here—So-ho, who has stole my Flambeaux?

(*Within.*) My Lady *Umbray's* Coach there—¹

FIFTH FOOTMAN. Hey! *Will*, pull up there. (*Exeunt Omnes.*)

Enter Lady Reveller *and* Alpiew, *her Woman.*

LADY REVELLER. My Lady *Raffle* is horridly out of humour at her ill Fortune, she lost 300 *l.*

ALPIEW. She has generally ill luck, yet her Inclination for Play is as strong as ever.—Did your Ladyship win, or lose, Madam?

LADY REVELLER. I won about 50 *l.*—prethee what shall we do, *Alpiew*? 'Tis a fine Morning, 'tis pity to go to Bed.

ALPIEW. What does your Ladyship think of a Walk in the Park?—The Park is pleasant in a Morning, the Air is so very sweet.

LADY REVELLER. I don't think so; the sweetness of the Park is at Eleven, when the Beau *Monde* makes their Tour† there, 'tis an unpolish'd Curiosity to walk when only Birds can see one.

ALPIEW. Bless me, Madam! Your Uncle—now for a Sermon of two Hours.

Enter Sir Richard Plainman, *in a Night-Gown as from Bed.*

SIR RICHARD PLAINMAN. So Niece! I find you're resolv'd to keep on your course of Life; I must be wak'd at Four with Coach, Coach, Chair, Chair; give over for shame, and Marry, Marry, Niece.

LADY REVELLER. Now would I forfeit the Heart of my next Admirer, to know the cause of this Reproach. Pray, Uncle,

---

1 Lady Umbray: probably pronounced Ombre, a popular trick-taking card game of the time.

explain† your self; for I protest I can't guess what Crime I have unhappily committed to merit this advice.

SIR RICHARD PLAINMAN. How can you look me in the Face, and ask me that Question? Can you that keep a Basset-Table, a publick Gaming-House, be insensible of the shame on't? I have often told you how much the vast concurse of People, which Day and Night make my House their Rendevouze, incommode my Health; your Apartment is a Parade for Men of all Ranks, from the Duke to the Fidler, and your Vanity thinks they all pay Devoir to your Beauty— but you mistake, every one has his several end in Meeting here, from the Lord to the Sharper, and each their separate Interest to Admire†—some Fools there may be, for there's seldom a crowd without.

LADY REVELLER. Malice—some Fools? I can't bear it.

ALPIEW. Nay, 'tis very affronting, truly Madam.

LADY REVELLER. Ay, is it not *Alpiew*?—Yet, now I think on't, 'tis the defect of Age to rail at the Pleasures of Youth, therefore I shall not disorder my Face with a frown about it. Ha, ha, I hope, Uncle you'l take peculiar care of my Cousin *Valeria*, in disposing of her according to the Breeding you have given her.

SIR RICHARD PLAINMAN. The Breeding I have given her! I would not have her have your Breeding, Mistress, for all the Wealth of *England*'s Bank; no, I bred† my Girl in the Country, a stranger to the Vices of this Town, and am resolv'd to Marry her to a Man of Honour, Probity and Courage.

LADY REVELLER. What the Sea Captain, Uncle? Faugh, I hate the smell of Pitch and Tarr; one that can Entertain one with nothing but Fire and Smoak, Larboard and Starboard, and t'other Bowl of Punch, ha, ha, ha.

ALPIEW. And for every fault that she commits he'll condemn her to the Bilboes,[1] ha, ha.

LADY REVELLER. I fancy my Cousin's Philosophy, and the Captain's Couragious Bluster, will make Angelick Harmony.

---

1 A moveable set of shackles, usually a long bar fastened to the ankles of prisoners and locked to the floor. In popular understanding this was often used for mutineers aboard ship.

SIR RICHARD PLAINMAN. Yes, Madam, sweeter Harmony than your Sept & Leva†[1] Fops, Rakes and Gamesters; give me the Man that serves my Country, that preserves both my Estate and Life—Oh, the glorious Name of Soldier; if I were Young, I'd go my self in Person, but as it is—

ALPIEW. You'll send your Daughter—

SIR RICHARD PLAINMAN. Yes, Minx, and a good Dowry with her, as a reward for Virtue like the Captains.

ALPIEW. But suppose, Sir, Mrs. *Valeria* should not like him?

SIR RICHARD PLAINMAN. I'll suppose no such thing, Mistress, she shall like him.

LADY REVELLER. Why, there 'tis now, indeed, Uncle, you're too positive.

SIR RICHARD PLAINMAN. And you too† Impertinent: Therefore I resolve to quit your House;† you shan't keep your Revels under the Roof where I am.[2]

ALPIEW. I'll have you to know, Sir, my Lady keeps no Revels beneath her Quality.

SIR RICHARD PLAINMAN. Hold your Tongue, Mrs. *Pert*, or I shall display your Quality in its proper Colours.

ALPIEW. I don't care, say your worst of me, and spare not; but for my Lady—my Lady's a Widdow, and Widdows are accountable to none for their Actions—Well, I shall have a Husband one of these days, and be a Widow too, I hope.

SIR RICHARD PLAINMAN. Not unlikely, for the Man will hang himself the next day, I warrant him.

ALPIEW. And if any, Uncle, pretends to controul my Actions—

SIR RICHARD PLAINMAN. He'd lose his labour, I'm certain—

ALPIEW. I'd treat him—

SIR RICHARD PLAINMAN. Don't provoke me, Houswife, don't.

LADY REVELLER. Be gone, and wait in the next Room. (*Ex. Alpiew.*)

---

1 A term from basset, meaning to win on a card three times and receive seven times your stake.

2 This implies that Sir Richard is staying at Lady Reveller's house. A few lines further on in this scene the reverse is implied. The second edition determines the house is Sir Richard's and Lady Reveller is the guest.

SIR RICHARD PLAINMAN. The Insolence of a Servant is a great Honour to the Lady, no doubt; but I shall find a way to humble you both.

LADY REVELLER. Lookee, Unkle, do what you can, I'm resolv'd to follow my own Inclinations.

SIR RICHARD PLAINMAN. Which infallibly carries you to Noise, Nonsense, Foppery and Ruin; but no matter, you shall out of my Doors, I'll promise you, my House shall no longer bear the Scandalous Name of a *Basset Table*: Husbands shall no more have cause to date their Ruin from my Door, nor cry there, there my Wife Gam'd my Estate away—Nor Children Curse my Posterity, for their Parents knowing my House.

LADY REVELLER. No more threatening, good Unkle, act as you please, but don't scold, or I shall be oblig'd to call *Alpiew* again.

SIR RICHARD PLAINMAN. Very well, very well, see what will come on't; the World will censure those that Game, and, in my Conscience, I believe not without Cause.
For she whose Shame, no good Advice can wake,
When Money's wanting, will her Virtue Stake. (Exit.)

LADY REVELLER. Advice! Ha, ha, ridiculous Advice. (*Enter Lady* Lucy.) No sooner rid of one mischief, but another follows—I foresee this is to be a day of Mortification, *Alpiew*.

Enter Alpiew.

ALPIEW. Madam.

LADY REVELLER. My Uncle's gone, you may come in, ha, ha, ha.

LADY LUCY. Fye, Cousin, does it become you to Laugh at those that give you Council for your good?

LADY REVELLER. For my good! Oh, mon cour?[1] Now cannot I Divine what 'tis, that I do more than the rest of the World, to deserve this blame.

ALPIEW. Nor I, for the Soul of me.

---

1 French, properly "mon coeur" meaning "my heart."

LADY LUCY. Shou'd all the rest of the World follow your Ladyship's Example, the order of Nature would be inverted, and every good, design'd by Heaven, become a Curse, Health and Plenty no longer would be known among us.—You cross the purpose of the Day and Night, you Wake when you should Sleep, and make all who have any dependence on you, Wake while you Repose.

LADY REVELLER. Bless me, may not any Person Sleep when they please?

LADY LUCY. No, there are certain Hours, that good Manners, Modesty and Health require your Care; for Example, disorderly Hours are neither Healthful nor Modest—And 'tis not Civil to make Company wait Dinner for your Dressing.

LADY REVELLER. Why, does any body Dine before four a Clock in *London*?[1] For my part I think it an Ill-bred Custom, to make my Appetite Pendulum to the Twelfth hour.

ALPIEW. Besides, 'tis out of Fashion to Dine by Day light, and so I told Sir *Richard* yesterday, Madam.

LADY LUCY. No doubt, but you did, Mrs. *Alpiew*; and then you entertain such a Train of People, Cousin, that my Lady *Reveller* is as noted as a publick Ordinary,[2] where every Fool with Money finds a Welcome.

LADY REVELLER. Would you have me shut my doors against my Friends—Now she is jealous of Sir *James Courtly*. (*Aside.*) Besides, is it possible to pass the Evenings without Diversions.

ALPIEW. No certainly—

LADY LUCY. I think the Play-house, the much more innocent and commendable Diversion.

LADY REVELLER. To be seen there every Night, in my Opinion, is more destructive to the Reputation.

LADY LUCY. Well, I had rather be noted every Night in the front Box, then, by my absence, once be suspected of Gaming; one

---

1   The *Tatler* for 14 December 1710 notes that later rising and dinning times were fashionable in London. This mode of modern life found the older generation "all of them fast asleep at the same hours that their daughters are busy at crimp and basset."

2   An Ordinary was an inn with meals provided at a fixed price. During this period at expensive ordinaries "dinner was usually followed by gambling; hence the term was often used as synonymous with gambling-house" (*OED*).

ruins my Estate and Character, the other diverts my Temper, and improves my Mind. Then you have such a number of Lovers.

LADY REVELLER. Oh *Cupid*, is it a Crime to have a number of Lovers? If it be, 'tis the pleasantest Crime in the World. A Crime that falls not every day, to every Woman's Lot.

LADY LUCY. I dare be positive every Woman does not wish it.

LADY REVELLER. Because wishes have no Effect, Cousin, ha, ha.

LADY LUCY. Methinks my Lord *Worthy's* Assiduity might have banish'd the admiring Crowd† by this time.

LADY REVELLER. Banish'd 'em? Oh, Mon cour! what pleasure is there in one Lover; 'tis like being seen always in one Suit of Cloaths; a Woman, with one Admirer, will ne'er be a Reigning Toast.

LADY LUCY. I am sure those that Encourage more, will never have the Character of a Reigning Virtue.

LADY REVELLER. I slight the malicious Censure of the Town, yet defy it to asperse my Vertue; Nature has given me a Face, a Shape, a Mein,[1] an Air for Dress, and Wit and Humour to subdue. And shall I lose my Conquest for a Name.

ALPIEW. Nay, and among the unfashionable sort of People too, Madam; for Persons of Breeding and Quality will allow that Gallantry and Virtue are not inseparable.

LADY LUCY. But Coquetry and Reputation are, and there is no difference† in the Eye of the World, between having really committed the Fault, and lying under the Scandal; for, my own part, I would take as much Care to preserve my Fame, as you would your Virtue.

LADY REVELLER. A little pains well serve you for that, Cousin; for I never once heard you nam'd—A Mortification would break my Heart, ha, ha.

LADY LUCY. 'Tis better never to be nam'd, than to be ill spoke of; but your Reflections shall not Disorder my Temper. I could wish, indeed, to convince you of your Error, because you share my Blood; but since I see the Vanity of the attempt, I shall desist.

---

1   Mien; a look or bearing that reveals character.

LADY REVELLER. I humbly thank your Ladiship.

ALPIEW. Oh! Madam, here's my Lord *Worthy*, Sir *James Courtly*, and Ensign *Lovely*, coming down; will your Ladyship see them?

LADY REVELLER. Now have I a strong Inclination to Engage Sir *James*, to discompose her Gravity; for if I have any Skill in Glances, she loves him—but then my Lord *Worthy* is so peevish since our late Quarrel, that I'm afraid to Engage the Knight in a Duel; besides, my Absence, I know, will teize him more, therefore, upon Consideration, I'le retire, Cousin *Lucy*; Good Morrow. I'le leave you to better Company, there's a Person at hand may prevent your Six-a-Clock Prayers. (*Exit.*)

LADY LUCY. Ha! Sir *James Courtly*—I must own I think him agreeable—but am sorry she believes I do. I'le not be seen; for if what I scarce know my self be grown so visible to her, perhaps, he too may Discover it, and then I am lost.
While in the Breast our Secrets close remain,
'Tis out of Fortunes power to give us Pain. (*Exit.*)

Enter Lord Worthy, *Sir* James, *Ensign* Lovely.†

SIR JAMES COURTLY. Ha! was not that Lady *Lucy*?

ENSIGN LOVELY. It was—ah, Sir *James*, I find your Heart is out of Order about that Lady, and my Lord *Worthy* languishes for Lady *Reveller*.

SIR JAMES COURTLY. And thou art sick for *Valeria*, Sir *Richard's* Daughter. A poor distressed Company of us.

ENSIGN LOVELY. 'Tis true, that little she-Philosopher has made me do Penance more heartily than ever my sins did; I deserve her by meer Dint of Patience. I have stood whole hours to hear her Assert that Fire cannot Burn, nor Water Drown, nor Pain Afflict, and forty ridiculous Systems—

SIR JAMES COURTLY. And all her Experiments on Frogs, Fish—and Flies, ha, ha, ha, without the least Contradiction.†

ENSIGN LOVELY. Contradiction, no, no, I allow'd all she said with undoubtedly, Madam,—I am of your mind, Madam, it must be so—natural Causes, &c.

SIR JAMES COURTLY. Ha, ha, ha, I think it is a supernatural cause which Enables thee to go thro' this Fatigue, if it were not to raise thy Fortune, I should think thee Mad to pursue her; but go on and prosper, nothing in my Power shall be wanting to assist you—My Lord *Worthy*—your Lordship is as Melancholy as a losing Gamester.

LORD WORTHY. Faith Gentlemen, I'm out of Humour, but I don't know at what.

SIR JAMES COURTLY. Why then I can tell you, for the very same reason that made your Lordship stay here to be Spectator of the very Diversion you hate—Gaming—the same Cause makes you uneasy in all Company, my Lady *Reveller*.

LORD WORTHY. Thou hast hit it, *James*, I confess I love her Person, but hate her Humours, and her way of Living; I have some reasons to believe I'm not indifferent to her, yet I despair of fixing her, her Vanity has got so much the Mistress of her Resolution; and yet her Passion for Gain surmounts her Pride, and lays her Reputation open to the World. Every Fool that has ready Money, shall dare to boast himself her very humble Servant; 'ds Death, when I could cut the Rascal's Throat.

SIR JAMES COURTLY. Your Lordship is even with her one Way, for you are as testy as she's vain, and as fond of an opportunity to Quarrel with her, as she of a Gaming Acquaintance; my Opinion is, my Lord, she'll ne're be won your Way.
To gain all Women there's a certain Rule,
If Wit should fail to please, then Act the Fool;
And where you find simplicity not take,
Throw off Disguises—and Profess the Rake;
Observe which Way their chiefest† Humours run,
They're by their own lov'd Cant† the surest Way undone.

LORD WORTHY. Thou'rt of a happy temper, Sir *James*, I wish I could be so too; but since I can't add to your Diversion, I'll take my leave, good Morrow, Gentlemen. (*Exit.*)

SIR JAMES COURTLY. This it is to have more Love than Reason about one; you and I *Lovely* will go on with Discretion, and yet I fear it's in Lady *Lucy's* Power to banish it.

ENSIGN LOVELY. I find Mrs. *Sago*, the Drugster's Wife's Interest, begins to shake, Sir *James*.

SIR JAMES COURTLY. And I fear her Love for Play begins to shake her Husband's Baggs too—faith, I am weary of that Intrigue,† lest I should be suspected to have a hand in his Ruin.

ENSIGN LOVELY. She did not lose much to Night, I believe; preethy, Sir *James*, what kind of a temper'd Woman is she? Has she Wit?

SIR JAMES COURTLY. That she has—A large Portion, and as much Cunning, or she could never have manag'd the old Fellow so nicely; she has a vast Passion for my Lady *Reveller*, and endeavours to mimick her in every thing—Not a sute of Cloaths, or a Top-knot,¹ that is not exactly the same with hers—then her Plots and Contrivances to supply these Expences, puts her continually upon the Rack; yet to give her her due, she has a fertile Brain that Way; but come, shall we go home and sleep two or three Hours, at Dinner I'll introduce you to Capt. *Hearty*, the Sea Officer, your Rival that is to be, he's just come to Town.

ENSIGN LOVELY. A powerful Rival, I fear, for Sir *Richard* resolves to Marry him to his Daughter; all my hopes lie† in her Arguments, and you know Philosophers are very positive—and if this Captain does but happen to Contradict one Whimsical Notion, the Poles will as soon join, as they Couple, and rather then yield, she would go to the Indies in search of *Dampier's* Ants.²

SIR JAMES COURTLY. Nay, she is no Woman if she Obeys.
Women like Tides with Passions Ebb and Flow,
And like them too, their source no Man can know.
To watch their Motions, is the safest Guide,
Who hits their Humour, Sails with Wind and Tide. (Exit.)

The End of the First ACT.

---

1 A ribbon worn on the top of the head.

2 William Dampier (1652-1715) published several accounts of voyages to the West Indies, with observations of the natural environment, including ants.

ACT II

Enter Buckle, *meeting Mrs.* Alpiew.

ALPIEW. Good Morrow.

BUCKLE. Good Morrow.

ALPIEW. Good Morrow, good Morrow, is that all your business
here; What means that Affected Look, as if you long'd to be
examin'd what's the Matter.

BUCKLE. The Capricio's of Love, *Madamoselle*; the Capricio's of
Love.

ALPIEW. Why—are you in Love?

BUCKLE. I—in Love! No, the Divel take me if ever I shall
be infected with that Madness, 'tis enough for one in a
Family to Fall under the whimsical Circumstances of that
Distemper. My Lord has a sufficient Portion for both;
here—here—here's a Letter for your Lady, I believe the
Contents are not so full of Stars and Darts, and Flames, as
they us'd to be.

ALPIEW. My Lady will not concern her self with your Lord, nor
his Letters neither, I can assure you that.

BUCKLE. So much the better, I'le tell him what you say—Have
you no more?

ALPIEW. Tell him it is not my fault, I have done as much for his
Service, as lay in my Power, till I put her in so great a Passion,
'tis impossible to Appease her.

BUCKLE. Very good—my Lord is upon the Square, I promise
ye, as much inraged as her Ladiship to the full. Well, Mrs.
Alpiew, to the longest Day of his Life he swears, never to
forget Yesterday's Adventure, that's given him perfect, perfect
Liberty.

ALPIEW. I believe so—What was it, pray?

BUCKLE. I'll tell you; 'twas a matter of Consequence, I assure
you, I've known Lovers part for a less Triffle by half.

ALPIEW. No Digressions,† but to the point, what was it?

BUCKLE. This—my Lord, was at the Fair with your Lady.

ALPIEW. What of that?

BUCKLE. In a Raffling-shop[1] she saw a young Gentleman, which she said was very handsome†—At the same time, my Lord, prais'd a young Lady; she redoubles her Commendations of the Beau—He enlarges on the Beauty of the Bell; their Discourse grew warm on the subject; they Pause; she begins again with the Perfections of the Gentleman; he ends with the same of the Lady; Thus they pursu'd† their Arguments, still finding such mighty Charms in their new Favourites, till they found one another so Ugly—so Ugly—that they parted with full Resolutions never to meet again.

ALPIEW. Ha, ha, ha, pleasant; well, if you have no more to tell me, adieu.

BUCKLE. Stay a Moment, I see my Lord coming, I thought he'd follow me. Oh, Lovers Resolutions—

Enter Lord Worthy.

LORD WORTHY. So, have you seen my Lady *Reveller*? (*To Buckle.*)

ALPIEW. My Lord—

LORD WORTHY. Ha! Mrs. *Alpiew.*

BUCKLE. There's your Lordship's Letter. (*Gives him his own Letter.*)

LORD WORTHY. An Answer! She has done me very much Honour.

ALPIEW. My Lord, I am commanded—

LORD WORTHY. Hold a little, dear Mrs. *Alpiew.* (*All this while he is opening the Letter, thinking it from the Lady.*)

BUCKLE. My Lord, she would not—

LORD WORTHY. Be quiet, I say—

ALPIEW. I am very sorry—

LORD WORTHY. But a moment—Ha, why, this is my own Letter.

---

1   A place where the gentry might play raffle, a dice game; *The Tatler* 59, 23-25 August 1709, is stern on the appearance of a raffling-shop at Hampstead. Edward Ward records one in *The London Spy* (London, 1703), I, 265.

BUCKLE. Yes, my Lord.

LORD WORTHY. Yes, my Lord—what, she'd not receive it then?

BUCKLE. No my Lord.

LORD WORTHY. How durst you stay so long.

ALPIEW. I beg your Lordship not to harbour an ill Opinion of me, I opposed her anger with my utmost Skill, prais'd all your Actions, all your Parts, but all in Vain.

LORD WORTHY. Enough, Enough, Madam, she has taken the best method in the World—Well, then we are ne'er to meet again?

ALPIEW. I know not that, my Lord—

LORD WORTHY. I am over-joy'd at it, by my Life I am, she has only prevented me; I came a purpose to break with her—

BUCKLE. (*Aside.*) Yes, so 'twas a sign by the pleasure you discover'd, in thinking she had writ to you.

LORD WORTHY. I suppose, she has entertain'd you with the Cause of this?

ALPIEW. No, my Lord, never mention'd a Syllable, only said, she had for ever done with you; and charg'd me, as I valued her favour, to receive no Message nor Letter, from you.

LORD WORTHY. May I become the very'st Wretch alive, and all the Ills imaginable† fall upon my Head, if I speak to her more; nay, ever think of her but with Scorn—Where is she now? (*Walks about.*)

ALPIEW. In her Dressing-room.

LORD WORTHY. There let her be, I am weary of her fantastick Humours, affected Airs, and unaccountable Passions.

BUCKLE. For half an Hour. (*Aside.*)

LORD WORTHY. Do you know what she's a doing?

ALPIEW. I believe, my Lord, trying on a Mantua;¹ I left her with Mrs. *Pleatwell*, and that us'd to hold her a great while, for the Woman is saucily Familiar with all the Quality, and tells her all the Scandal.

---

1 A mantua was a loose gown without stays.

LORD WORTHY. And conveys Letters upon occasion; 'tis tack'd to their Professions[1]—But, my Lady *Reveller* may do what she pleases, I am no more her Slave, upon my Word; I have broke my Chain—She has not been out then since she Rose?

ALPIEW. No, my Lord.

LORD WORTHY. Nay, if she has, or has not, 'tis the same thing to me; she may go to the end of the World, if she will; I shan't take any pains to follow her—Whose Footman was that I met?

ALPIEW. I know not, my Lord, we have so many come with How-dee's, I ne'er mind them.

LORD WORTHY. You are uneasy, Child, come, I'll not detain you, I have no curiosity, I protest I'm satisfied if she's so, I assure ye, let her despise me, let her hate me, 'tis all one, adieu. (*Going.*)

ALPIEW. My Lord, your Servant.

LORD WORTHY. Mrs. *Alpiew*, let me beg one favour of you, (*Turns back.*) not to say I was here.

ALPIEW. I'll do just as you please, my Lord.

LORD WORTHY. Do that then, and you'll oblige me. (*Is going, and comes back often.*)†

ALPIEW. I will.

LORD WORTHY. Don't forget.

ALPIEW. Your Lordship may depend upon me.

LORD WORTHY. Hold, now I think on't—Pray tell her you did see me, do you hear?

ALPIEW. With all my Heart.

LORD WORTHY. Tell her how indifferent she is to me in every respect.

ALPIEW. I shan't fail.

LORD WORTHY. Tell her every thing, just as I exprest it to you.

ALPIEW. I will.

---

1 "Tacked" here is a metaphor for the seamstress's double function as needlewoman and courier. There may be a further, political allusion, as in 1704 high-church Anglicans and Tories tried to tack a bill to suppress Occasional Conformity (where dissenters qualified for office by taking occasional communion within the Anglican church) onto the Land Tax Bill. The move was defeated, but tacking was regarded as a devious or underhanded activity.

LORD WORTHY. Adieu. (*Going.*)

ALPIEW. Your Servant.

LORD WORTHY. Now, I think on't Mrs. *Alpiew*, I have a great mind she shou'd know my Sentiments from my own Mouth.

ALPIEW. Nay, my Lord, I can't promise you that.

LORD WORTHY. Why?

ALPIEW. Because she has expresly forbid your admittance.

LORD WORTHY. I'd speak but one Word with her.

ALPIEW. Impossible.

LORD WORTHY. Pugh, prethee do, let me see her. (*Intreating Mrs Alpiew.*)

BUCKLE. So now, all this mighty rage ends in a begging Submission.

LORD WORTHY. Only tell her I'm here.

ALPIEW. Why should you desire me to meet her Anger, my Lord?

LORD WORTHY. Come, you shall oblige me once. (*Puts a Ring upon her Finger.*)

ALPIEW. Oh, dear, my Lord, you have such a command over your Servant, I can refuse nothing. (*Exit.*)

LORD WORTHY. Have you been at the Goldsmiths about the Bills, for I am fix'd on Travelling.

BUCKLE. Your Lordship's so disturb'd, you have forgot you Countermanded me, and send me hither.

LORD WORTHY. True.

Enter Mrs. Alpiew.

ALPIEW. Just as I told your Lordship, she fell in a most violent Passion, at the bare mention of your Name; tell him, said she, in a heroick Strain, I'll never see him more, and command him to quit that Room, 'cause I'm coming to't.

LORD WORTHY. Tyrant, curse on my Follies, she knows her Power; well, I hope, I may walk in the Gallery; I would speak with her Uncle.

ALPIEW. To be sure, my Lord. (*Exit Lord* Worthy.)

BUCKLE. Learn, Mistress, learn, you may come to make me Mad in time, ha, ha, ha.

ALPIEW. Go Fool, follow your Lord. (*Exit.* Buckle.)

Enter Lady Reveller.

LADY REVELLER. Well, I'll swear, *Alpiew*, you have given me
the Vapours for all Day.

ALPIEW. Ah! Madam, if you had seen him, you must have had
Compassion: I would not have such a Heart of Adamant for the
World; poor Lord, sure you have the strangest Power over him.

LADY REVELLER. Silly—one often Fancies one has Power,
when one has none at all; I'll tell thee *Alpiew*, he vex'd me
strangely before this grand Quarrel; I was at *Picquet*[1] with my
Lady *Love-Witt* four Nights ago, and bid him read me a new
Copy of Verses, because, you know, he never Plays, and I did
not well know what to do with him; he had scarce begun,
when I being eager at a Pique, he rose up and said, he believ'd I
love'd the Musick of my own Voice, crying Nine and Twenty,
Threescore, better than the sweetest Poetry in the Universe,
and abruptly left us.

ALPIEW. A great Crime, indeed, not to read when People are at
a Game they are oblig'd to talk to all the while.

LADY REVELLER. Crime, yes, indeed was it, for my Lady loves
Poetry better than Play, and perhaps before the Poem had
been done had lost her Money to me. But, I wonder, *Alpiew*,
by what Art 'tis you engage me in this Discourse, why shou'd
I talk of a Man that's utterly my Aversion—Have you heard
from Mrs. *Sago* this Morning?

ALPIEW. Certainly, Madam, she never fails; she has sent your
Ladiship the finest Cargo made up of Chocolate, Tea,
Montifiasco Wine, and 50 Rarities beside, with something
to remember me, good Creature, that she never forgets.
Well, indeed Madam, she is the best natur'd Woman in
the World; it grieves me to think what Sums she loses at
Play.

---

1   A card game for two players, where players score points for runs, sets, and taking
tricks. Lady Reveller's excitement about scoring "nine-and-twenty, threescore" suggests that she scored a *repique,* where reaching thirty before your opponent scores
brings you an extra sixty points, and probably the game.

LADY REVELLER. Oh fye, she must, a Citizen's Wife is not to be endur'd amongst Quality; had she not Money, 'twere impossible to receive her—

ALPIEW. Nay, indeed, I must say that of you Women of Quality, if there is but Money enough, you stand not upon Birth or Reputation, in either Sex; if you did, so many Sharpers of *Covent-Garden*, and Mistresses of St. *James's* would not be daily admitted.

LADY REVELLER. Peace, Impertinence, you take strange Freedoms. (*Enter* Valeria† *running.*) Why in such hast Cousin Valeria. (*Stopping her.*)

VALERIA. Oh! dear Cousin, don't stop me, I shall lose the finest Insect for Desection, a huge Flesh Fly, which Mr. *Lovely* sent me just now, and opening the Box to try the Experiment away it flew.

LADY REVELLER. I am glad the poor Fly escap'd; will you never be weary of these Whimsies?

VALERIA. Whimsies! natural Philosophy† a Whimsy! Oh, the unlearn'd World.

LADY REVELLER. Ridiculous Learning?

ALPIEW. Ridiculous, indeed, for Women; Philosophy suits† our Sex, as Jack Boots[1] would do.

VALERIA. Custom would bring them as much in Fashion as Furbeloes,[2] and Practice would make us as Valiant as e're a Hero of them all; the Resolution is in the Mind,—Nothing can enslave that.

LADY REVELLER. My Stars! this Girl will be Mad, that's certain.

VALERIA. Mad ! so *Nero* Banish'd Philosophers from *Rome*, and the first Discoverer of the *Antipodes* was Condemn'd for a Heretick.[3]

LADY REVELLER. In my Conscience, *Alpiew*, this pritty Creature's spoil'd. Well, Cousin, might I Advise, you should bestow your Fortune in Founding a College for the Study of Philosophy, where none but Women should be admitted, and

---

1 Long military boots, usually worn by cavalry soldiers.

2 Ornamental flounces on a dress or petticoat.

3 Nero (ca. 15-68), the Roman emperor, was celebrated in Nathaniel Lee's *The Tragedy of Nero* (1675). He was responsible for Seneca's death, after the latter's rebellion.

to Immortalize your Name, they should be call'd *Valerians*, ha, ha, ha.[1]

VALERIA. What you make a Jest of, I'de Execute, were Fortune in my Power.

ALPIEW. All Men would not be Excluded, the handsome† Ensign, Madam.

LADY REVELLER. In Love? Nay, there's no Philosophy against Love, *Solon* for that.[2]

VALERIA. Pisha, no more of this Triffling Subject; Cousin, will you believe there's any thing without Gall?†

LADY REVELLER. I am satisfy'd I have one, when I lose at Play, or see a Lady Addrest when I am by, and 'tis equal to me, whether the rest of Creation have or not.

VALERIA. Well, but I'le convince you then, I have dissected my Dove—and positively I think the Vulgar Notion true, for I could find none.

LADY REVELLER. Oh, Barbarous; kill'd your pritty Dove! (*Starting.*)

VALERIA. Kill'd it! Why, what did you Imagine I bred it up for? Can Animals, Insects or Reptils, be put to a Noble use, than to improve our Knowledge? Cousin, I'll give you this Jewel for your *Italian* Grey-hound.

LADY REVELLER. What, to Cut to Pieces? Oh, horrid! he had need be a Soldier that ventures on you, for my part, I should Dream of nothing but Incision, Dissection and amputation, and always fancy the Knife at my Throat.

Enter Servant.

SERVANT. Madam, here's Sir *Richard*, and a—

VALERIA. A—What, is it an Accident, a Substance, a Material Being, or, a Being of Reason?

SERVANT. I don't know what you call a Material Being; it is a Man.

VALERIA. P'sha, a Man, that's nothing.

---

1 This is a mocking reference to Mary Astell's suggestion in *A Serious Proposal to the Ladies* (1694); see Appendix A1.

2 Solon (ca. 638-558 BCE) was an Athenian lawmaker who also wrote love poetry.

LADY REVELLER. She'll prove by and by out of *Descartes*,† that we are all Machines.[1]

(*Enter Sir* Richard, *and Capt.* Firebrand.)[2]

ALPIEW. Oh, Madam, do you see who observes you? My Lord walking in the Gallery, and every Minute gives a Peep.

LADY REVELLER. Does he so? I'll fit him for Eves-dropping—

SIR RICHARD PLAINMAN. Sir, I like the Relation you have given me of your Naval Expedition, your Discourse speaks you a Man fit for the Sea.

CAPTAIN HEARTY. You had it without a flourish, Sir *Richard*, my Word is this, I hate the *French*, Love a handsome Woman, and a Bowl of Punch.

VALERIA. Very Blunt.

SIR RICHARD PLAINMAN. This is my Daughter, Captain, a Girl of sober Education; she understands nothing of Gaming, Parks and Plays.

ALPIEW. But wanting these Diversions, she has supply'd the Vacancy with greater Follies. (*Aside.*)

CAPTAIN HEARTY. A Tite little Frigate, (*Salutes her*) Faith, I think, she looks like a freshman Sea-Sick—but here's a Gallant Vessel—with all her Streamers out, Top and Top Gallant[3]—with your leave, Madam, (*Salutes her*) who is that Lady, Sir *Richard*?

SIR RICHARD PLAINMAN. 'Tis a Niece of mine, Captain— tho' I am sorry she is so, she values nothing that does not spend their days at their Glass, and their Nights at *Basset*, such who ne'er did good to their Prince, nor Country, except their Taylor, Peruke-maker,[4] and Perfumer.

---

1 René Descartes (1596-1650), philosopher. One of his central arguments was that the mind and body were distinct entities, and that animals were only mechanical beings, without a soul; see his "Letters to Henry More," *The Philosophical Writings of Descartes*, ed. Cottingham, Stoothoff, Murdoch, and Kenny (Cambridge: Cambridge UP, 1991), III, 365-66.

2 Actually Captain Hearty. This textual "slip" suggests that this figure began life as an allusion to Farquhar's sea captain Fireball in *Sir Harry Wildair* (1671), played by Johnson, who acted Sago in *The Basset Table*.

3 Captain Hearty uses nautical terms to describe Lady Reveller, comparing the ribbons placed high in her hair or wig to sails on the highest point of the topmast.

4 Wig maker.

LADY REVELLER. Fy, fy, Sir, believe him not, I have a Passion, an extream Passion, for a Hero—especially if he belongs to the Sea; methinks he has an Air so Fierce, so Piercing, his very Looks commands Respect from his own Sex, and all the Hearts of ours.

SIR RICHARD PLAINMAN. The Divel—Now, rather than let another Female have a Man to her self, she'll make the first Advances. (*Aside.*)

CAPTAIN HEARTY. Ay, Madam, we are preferr'd by you fine Ladies sometimes before the sprucer Sparks—there's a Conveniency in't; a fair Wind, and we hale out, and leave you Liberty and Money, two things the most acceptable to a Wife in Nature.

LADY REVELLER. Oh! ay, it is so pretty to have one's Husband gone Nine Months of the Twelve, and then to bring one home fine China, fine Lace, fine Muslin, and fine Indian Birds, and a thousand Curiosities.

SIR RICHARD PLAINMAN. No, no, Nine is a little too long, six would do better for one of your Constitution, Mistress.†

CAPTAIN HEARTY. Well, Madam, what think you of a cruising Voyage towards the Cape of Matrimony, your Father designs me for the Pilot, if you agree to it, we'll hoist Sail immediately.

VALERIA. I agree with any thing dictated by good Sense, and comprehended within the Borders of Elocution. The converse† I hold with your Sex is only to improve and cultivate the Notions of my Mind.

SIR RICHARD PLAINMAN. What the Devil is she going upon now? (*Aside.*)

VALERIA. I presume you're† a Mariner, Sir—

CAPTAIN HEARTY. I have the Honour to bear the Queen's Commission, Madam.

VALERIA. Pray, speak properly, positively, Laconically and Naturally.

LADY REVELLER. So she has given him a Broadside already.

CAPTAIN HEARTY. Laconically? Why, why, what is your Daughter? Sir *Richard*, ha.

SIR RICHARD PLAINMAN. May I be reduc'd to Wooden-Shoes, if I can tell you, the Devil;[1] had I liv'd near a College, the Haunts of some Pedant† might have brought this Curse upon me; but to have got my Estate in the City, and to have a Daughter run Mad after Philosophy, I'll ne'er suffer it in the rage I am in, I'll throw all the Books and Mathematical Instruments out of the Window.

LADY REVELLER. I dare say, Uncle, you have shook hands with Philosophy—for I am sure you have banish'd Patience, ha, ha, ha.

SIR RICHARD PLAINMAN. And you Discretion—By all my hatred for the *French*, they'll drive me Mad; Captain, I'll expect you in the next Room, and you Mrs. *Laconick*, with your Philosophy at your Tail. (*Exit.*)

LADY REVELLER. Shan't I come too, Uncle, ha, ha.

CAPTAIN HEARTY. By *Neptune*, this is a kind of a whimsical Family; well, Madam, what was you going to say to positively and properly, and so forth?

VALERIA. I would have ask'd you, Sir, if ever you had the curiosity to inspect a Mermaid—Or if you are convinc'd there is a World in every Star[2]—We, by our Telliscopes, find Seas, Groves and Plains, and all that; but what they are Peopled with, there's the Query.[3]

CAPTAIN HEARTY. Let your next Contrivance be how to get thither, and then you'll know a World in every Star— Ha, ha, she's fitter for *Moorfields*[4] than Matrimony, pray,

---

1 A political reference indicating Sir Richard Plainman's hatred of the French. Clogs or wooden shoes were an emblem of French slavery, and were carried in electoral processions and protests in the early 1700s; see the Whig newspaper, *The Flying Post*, 30 October 1714.

2 A reference perhaps to John Milton's *Paradise Lost* (1667), Book 7, lines 621-22: "every star perhaps a world/ Of destined habitation."

3 This was a hotly debated scientific question of the period, popularized by Bernard de Fontenelle's *A Discourse on the Plurality of Worlds* (1686), aimed at a female readership and was translated by Aphra Behn as *A Discovery of New Worlds* (1688). Centlivre wrote a poem in the front of Anne Oldfield's copy of Behn's translation.

4 Hospital for the mentally ill, London. The Hospital of St. Mary's Bethlehem, or Bedlam, the only hospital in England for the mentally ill, was relocated to a purpose-built structure in Moorfields in 1675. To recoup costs it charged an entrance fee for visitors to view the inmates.

Madam, are you always infected, full and change, with this Distemper?

VALERIA. How has my reason err'd, to hold converse with an irrational Being—Dear, dear Philosophy, what immense pleasures dwell in thee!

Enter Servant.

SERVANT. Madam, *John*, has got the Fish you sent him in search of.

VALERIA. Is it alive?

SERVANT. Yes, Madam.

VALERIA. Your Servant, your Servant, I would not lose the Experiment for any thing, but the tour of the new World. (*Exit.*)

CAPTAIN HEARTY. Ha, ha, ha, is your Ladiship troubled with these Vagaries too; is the whole House possest?

LADY REVELLER. Not I, Captain, the speculative faculty is not my Talent; I am for the practick, can listen† all Day, to hear you talk of Fire, substantial Fire, Rear and Front, and Line of Battle—admire a Seaman, hate the *French*—love a Bowl of Punch? Oh, nothing so agreeable as your Conversation, nothing so Jaunty as a Sea Captain.

ALPIEW. So this engages him to Play,—If he has either Manners or Money. (*Aside.*)

CAPTAIN HEARTY. Ay, give me the Woman that can hold me tack in my own Dialect—She's Mad too, I suppose, but I'll humour her a little. (*Aside.*) Oh, Madam, not a fair Wind, nor a rich Prize, nor Conquest o're my Enemies, can please like you; accept my Heart without Capitulation—'Tis yours, a Prisoner at Discretion. (*Kisses her Hand.*)

Enter Lord Worthy.

LORD WORTHY. Hold, Sir, you must there contend with me; the Victory is not so easy as you imagine.

LADY REVELLER. Oh fye, my Lord, you won't fight for one you hate and despise? I may trust you with the Captain, ha, ha, ha. (*Exit.*)

CAPTAIN HEARTY. This must be her Lover—And he is Mad another way; this is the most unaccountable Family I ever met with. (*Aside.*) Lookye, Sir, what you mean by contending I know not; but I must tell you, I don't think any Woman I have seen since I came ashoar worth Fighting for. The Philosophical Gimcrack[1] I don't value of a Cockle Shell—And am too well acquainted with the danger of Rocks and Quick-sands to steer into t'others Harbour.

LORD WORTHY. He has discover'd her already; I, only I, am blind. (*Aside.*)

CAPTAIN HEARTY. But , Sir, if you have a mind to a Breathing, here tread upon my Toe, or speak but one Word in favour of the *French*, or against the Courage of our Fleet, and my Sword will start of its self, to do its Master, and my Country, Justice.

LORD WORTHY. How ridiculous do I make my self—Pardon me, Sir, you are in the right. I confess I scarce knew what I did.

CAPTAIN HEARTY. I thought so, poor Gentleman, I pitty him; this is the effect of Love on shoar—When do we hear of a Tarr in these fits, longer then the first fresh Gale—Well, I'll into Sir *Richard*. Eat with him, Drink with him: but to Match into his Generation, I'd as soon Marry one of his Daughters Mermaids. (*Exit.*)

LORD WORTHY. Was ever Man so stupid as my self? But I will rouse from this Lethargick Dream, and seek elsewhere what is deny'd at home, absence may restore my Liberty.

Enter Mr. Sago.

MR. SAGO. Pray, my Lord, did you see my *Keecky.*[2]

LORD WORTHY. *Keecky*, what's that?

MR. SAGO. My Wife, you must know, I call her *Keecky*, ha, ha.

LORD WORTHY. Not I, indeed—

MR. SAGO. Nay, pray my Lord, ben't angry, I only want her, to tell her what a Present of fine Wine is sent her just now; and

---

1   "A showy, unsubstantial thing ... a knick-knack" (*OED*); also, a theatrical reference to Sir Nicholas Gimcrack, the crazed philosopher of Thomas Shadwell's *The Virtuoso* (1676).

2   An affectionate term from keek, to peep, used by children in hide and seek, "keek-bo."

ha, ha, ha, ha, what makes me Laugh—Is that, no Soul can tell from whence it comes.

LORD WORTHY. Your Wife knows, no doubt.

MR. SAGO. No more than my self, my Lord—We have often Wine and Sweetmeats; nay, whole pieces of Silk, and the duce take me, if she could devise from whence; nay, sometimes she has been for sending them back again, but I cry'd, whose a Fool then—

LORD WORTHY. I'm sure thou art one in perfection, and to me insupportable. (*Going.*)

MR. SAGO. My Lord, I know your Lordship has the Priviledge of this House, pray do me the Kindness if you find my Wife to send her out to me. (*Exit* Lord.)

I ne'er saw so much of this Lord's Humour before; he is very Surly Methinks—Adod[1] there are some Lords of my Wives Acquaintance, as Civil and Familiar with me, as I am with my Journeyman—Oh! here she comes.

Enter Mrs. Sago *and* Alpiew.

MRS. SAGO. Oh Puddy,[2] see what my Lady *Reveller* has presented me withal.

MR. SAGO. Hey Keecky, why sure you Rise—as the saying is, for at Home there's Four Hampers of Wine sent ye.

MRS. SAGO. From whence, Dear Puddy?

MR. SAGO. Nay, there's the Jest, neither you nor I know. I offer'd the Rogue that brought it a Guinea to tell from whence it came, and he Swore he durst not.

MRS. SAGO. No, if he had I'd never have Employ'd him again. (*Aside.*)

MR. SAGO. So I gave him Half a Crown, and let him go.

MRS. SAGO. It comes very Opportunely pray Puddy send a Couple of the Hampers to my Lady *Reveller* as a small Acknowledgement for the Rich Present she has made me.

---

1 Short for "Ah God," one of many variants employed by playwrights to escape the charge of using blasphemous language on stage. This particular coinage used by Centlivre is intended to mark Sago's lower class status.

2 Centlivre was fond of using Puddy in babytalk between characters. *The Artifice* (1722) reuses the verbal tick between its citizen-class characters.

MR. SAGO. With all my Heart, my Jewel, my Precious.

MRS. SAGO. Puddy, I am strangely oblig'd to Mrs. *Alpiew*, do Puddy, do, Dear Puddy.

MR. SAGO. What?

MRS. SAGO. Will ye, then? Do, Dear Puddy, do, lend me a Guinea to give to her, do. (*Hanging upon him in a Wheedling Tone.*)

MR. SAGO. P'shaw, you are always wanting Guineas, I'll send her Half a Pound of *Tea*, Keecky.

MRS. SAGO. *Tea*—sha—she Drinks Ladies *Tea*; do, Dear Pudd, do; can you deny Keecky now?

MR. SAGO. Well, well, there. (*Gives it her.*)

MRS. SAGO. Mrs. *Alpiew*, will you please to lay the Silk by for me, till I send for it, and accept of That?

ALPIEW. Your Servant Madam, I'll be careful of it.

MRS. SAGO. Thank ye, Borrow as much as you can on't, Dear *Alpiew*. (*Aside to her.*)

ALPIEW. I warrant you, Madam. (*Exit.*)

MRS. SAGO. I must Raise a Summ for *Basset* against Night.

MR. SAGO. Preethy Keecky, what kind of Humour'd Man is Lord *Worthy*? I did but ask him if he saw thee, and I Thought he would snapp'd my Nose off.

MRS. SAGO. Oh a meer Woman, full of Spleen and Vapours, he and I never agree.

MR. SAGO. Adod, I thought so—I guess'd† he was none of thy Admirers—Ha, ha, ha, why there's my Lord *Courtall*, and my Lord *Horncit*, bow down to the Ground to me wherever they meet me.

Enter Alpiew.

ALPIEW. Madam, Madam, the *Goldsmith* has sent in the Plate.

MRS. SAGO. Very well, take it along with the Silk. (*Aside to her.*)

ALPIEW. Here's the *Jeweller*; Madam, with the Diamond Ring, but he don't seem willing to leave it without Money. (*Exit* Alpiew.)

MRS. SAGO. Humph? I have a sudden Thought, bid him stay and bring me the Ring—Now for the Art of Wheedling.—

MR. SAGO. What are you Whispering about? Ha? Precious.—

MRS. SAGO. Mrs. *Alpiew* says, a Friend of her has a Diamond Ring to Sell, a great Penny-worth and I know you love a Bargain Puddy.

Enter Alpiew, *gives her the Ring.*

MR. SAGO. P'shaw, I don't care for Rings; it may be a Bargain, and it may not; and I can't spare Money; I have Paid for a Lot this Morning; consider Trade must go forward, Lambkin.

ALPIEW. See how it Sparkles.

MRS. SAGO. Nay, Puddy, if it be not Worth your Money I don't desire you to Buy it; but don't it become my Finger, Puddy? See now.—

MR. SAGO. Ah! that Hand, that Hand it was which first got hold of my Heart; well what's the Price of it; Ha, I am ravish'd to see it upon Keecky's Finger.—

MRS. SAGO. What did he say the Price was? (*To* Alpiew.)

ALPIEW. Two Hundred *Guineas*, Madam. (*Aside to Mrs.* Sago.)

MRS. SAGO. Threescore Pound, Dear Pudd, the Devils in't if he won't give that. (*Aside.*)

MR. SAGO. Threescore Pounds? Why 'tis Worth a Hundred Child, Richly—'tis Stole—'tis Stole.—

ALPIEW. Stole? I'd have you know the Owner is my Relation, and has been as great a Merchant as any in *London*, but has had the Misfortune to have his Ships fall into the Hands of the *French*, or he'd not have parted with it at such a Rate; it Cost him Two Hundred *Guineas.*

MRS. SAGO. I believe as much, indeed 'tis very fine.

MR. SAGO. So it is Keecky, and that Dear little Finger shall have it to let me Bite it; a little Tiny bit.—(*Bites her Finger.*)

MRS. SAGO. Oh! Dear Pudd, you Hurt me.

MR. SAGO. Here—I han't so much Money about me, but there's† a Bill, Lambkin—there now, you'll Buss poor Puddy now, won't you?

MRS. SAGO. Buss him—yes, that I will agen, and agen, and agen, Dear Pudd. (*Flies about his Neck.*)

MR. SAGO. You'll go Home with Puddy now to Dinner, won't you?

MRS. SAGO. Yes—a—Dear Puddy, if you desire it—I will—but—a—

MR. SAGO. But what?

MRS. SAGO. But I promis'd my Lady *Reveller* to Dine with her, Deary—do, let me Pudd—I'll Dine with you to Morrow-day.

ALPIEW. Nay, I'm sure my Lady won't Eat a bit if she don't stay.

MR. SAGO. Well, they are so Fond of my Wife, by Keecky, show me the Little Finger agen—Oh! Dear Little Finger, by by Keecky.

MRS. SAGO. By own Pudd—Here *Alpiew* give him his Ring agen, I have my End, tell him 'tis too† Dear. (*Aside.*)

ALPIEW. But what will you say when Mr. *Sago* misses it.

MRS. SAGO. I'll say—that it was two big for my Finger, and I lost it; 'tis but a Crying-bout, and the good Man melts into Pity—

I'th' Married State, this only Bliss we find,
An Easie Husband to our Wishes kind.
I've Gain'd my Point, Replenish'd Purse once more,
Oh! cast me Fortune on the Winning Shore.
Now let me Gain what I have Lost before.

(*Exit.*)

ACT III

The Scene draws, and discovers Valeria *with Books upon a Table, a Microscope, putting a Fish upon it, several Animals lying by.*

VALERIA. Sha! Thou fluttering Thing.—So now I've fix'd it.

Enter Alpiew.

ALPIEW. Madam, here's Mr. *Lovely*; I have introduc'd him as One of my Lady's Visitors, and brought him down the Back-stairs.
VALERIA. I'm oblig'd to you, he comes opportunely.

Enter Lovely.

Oh! Mr. *Lovely*, come, come here, look through this Glass, and see how the Blood Circulates in the Tale of this Fish.
ENSIGN LOVELY. Wonderful! but it Circulates prettier in this Fair Neck.
VALERIA. Pshaw—be quiet—I'll show you a Curiosity, the greatest that ever Nature made—(*Opens a Box*) in opening a Dog the other Day I found this Worm.
ENSIGN LOVELY. Prodigious! 'tis the Joint-Worm, which the Learned talk of so much.
VALERIA. Ay, the *Lumbricus Latus*, or *Foescia*, as *Hippocrates* calls it, or Vulgarly in *English* the Tape-Worm.—*Thudaeus* tells us of One of these Worms found in a Human Body 200 Foot long, without Head or Tail.[1]

---

[1] Edward Tyson (1651-1708) read his *Lumbricus Latus, or a Discourse Read before the Royal Society of the Joynted Worm*, and his study on the round worm, *Lumbricus teres* (1683), and published them with illustrations of dissections in *Philosophical Transactions* (1683-1775), 13, 113-44. It is from these publications that Centlivre directly copies the reference to Hippocrates (ca. 470-380 BCE), the Greek physician, and the story of the large tapeworm taken from a human seen by Thaddaeus Dunus. Valeria's interest in *Lumbricus teres Intestinalis* and her observations on joints and mouths come from the same source.

ENSIGN LOVELY. I wish they be not got into thy Brain. (*Aside.*) Oh you Charm me with these Discoveries.

VALERIA. Here's another Sort of Worm call'd *Lumbricus teres Intestinalis*.

ENSIGN LOVELY. I think the First you show'd me the greatest Curiosity.

VALERIA. 'Tis very odd, really, that there should be every Inch a Joint, and ever Joint a Mouth.—Oh the profound Secrets of Nature!

ENSIGN LOVELY. 'Tis strangely Surprizing.—But now let me be heard, for mine's the Voice of Nature too; methinks you neglect your self, the most Perfect Piece of all her Works.

VALERIA. Why? What Fault do you find in me?

ENSIGN LOVELY. You have not Love enough; that Fire would Consume and Banish all Studies but its own; your Eyes wou'd Sparkle, and spread I know not what, of Lively and Touching, o'er the whole Face; this Hand, when Press'd by him you Love, would Tremble to your Heart.

VALERIA. Why so it does—have I not told you Twenty Times I Love you,—for I hate Disguise; your Temper being Adapted to mine, gave my Soul the First Impression;—you know my Father's Positive,—but do not believe he shall Force me to any Thing that does not Love Philosophy.

ENSIGN LOVELY. But that Sea Captain *Valeria*.

VALERIA. If he was a Whale he might give you Pain, for I should long to Dissect him; but as he is a Man, you have no Reason to Fear him.

ENSIGN LOVELY. Consent then to Fly with me.

VALERIA. What, and leave my Microscope, and all my Things, for my Father to break in Pieces.

SIR RICHARD PLAINMAN. *Valeria, Valeria.* (*Within.*)

VALERIA. Oh Heav'ns! Oh Heav'ns! he is coming up the Back-stairs. What shall we do?

ENSIGN LOVELY. Humph, ha, cann't you put me in that Closet there?

VALERIA. Oh no, I han't the Key.

ENSIGN LOVELY. I'll run down the Great Stairs, let who will see me. (*Going.*)

VALERIA. Oh no, no, no, no, not for your Life;—here, here, here, get under this Tub. (*Throws out some Fish in Hast, and Turns the Tub over him.*)
Sir, I'm here.

Enter Sir Richard.

SIR RICHARD PLAINMAN. What, at your Whims—and Whirligigs, ye Baggage? I'll out at Window with them. (*Throwing away the Things.*)
VALERIA. Oh Dear Father, save my *Lumbricus Latus.*
SIR RICHARD PLAINMAN. I'll Lamprey[1] and Latum you; what's that I wonder? Ha? Where the Devil got you Names that your Father don't understand? Ha? (*Treads upon them.*)
VALERIA. Oh my poor Worm! Now have you destroy'd a Thing, that, for ought I know, *England* cann't produce again.
SIR RICHARD PLAINMAN. What is it good for? Answer me that?—What's this Tub here for? Ha? (*Kicks it.*)
VALERIA. What shall I do now?—it is, a 'tis a—Oh Dear Sir! Don't touch the Tub,—for there's a Bear's Young Cub that I have brought for Dissection,—but I dare not touch it till the Keeper comes.
SIR RICHARD PLAINMAN. I'll Cub you, and Keeper you, with a Vengeance to you; is my Money laid out on Bears Cubs?—I'll drive out your Cub.—(*Opens the Door, stands at a Distance off, and with his Cane, lifts up the Tub.* Lovely *rises.*)
ENSIGN LOVELY. Oh the Devil discover'd, your Servant Sir. (*Exit.*)
SIR RICHARD PLAINMAN. Oh! your Servant Sir—What is this your Bear Cub? Ha Mistress? His Taylor has lick'd him into Shape I find.—What did this Man do here? Ha Huswife?—I doubt you have been studying Natural Philosophy with a Vengeance.
VALERIA. Indeed, Sir, he only brought me a strange Fish, and hearing your Voice, I was afraid you should be Angry, and so that made me hide him.

---

1 An eel-like fish.

SIR RICHARD PLAINMAN. A Fish,—'tis the Flesh I fear; I'll have you Married to'Night.—I believe this Fellow was the Beggarly Ensign, who never March'd further than from *Whitehall* to the *Tower*, who wants your Portion to make him a Brigadier, without ever seeing a Battel[1]—Huswife, ha—tho' your Philosophical Cant, with a Murrain[2] to you—has put the Captain out of Conceit, I have a Husband still for you;—come along, come along, I'll send the Servants to clear this Room of your Bawbles,—(*pulls her off*) I will so.

VALERIA. But the Servants won't, Old Gentleman, that's my Comfort still. (*Exit.*)

Re-enter Lovely.

ENSIGN LOVELY. I'm glad they are gone, for the Duce take me if I cou'd hit the Way out.

Enter Sir James.

SIR JAMES COURTLY. Ha—Ensign! luckily met; I have been Labouring for you, and I hope done you a Piece of Service. Why, you look surpriz'd.

ENSIGN LOVELY. Surpriz'd! so wou'd you, Sir *Harry*,[3] if you had been whelm'd under a Tub, without Room to Breath.

SIR JAMES COURTLY. Under a Tub! Ha, ha, ha.

ENSIGN LOVELY. 'Twas the only Place of Shelter.

SIR JAMES COURTLY. Come, come, I have a better Prospect, the Captain is a very Honest Fellow, and thinks if you can

---

1 Sir Richard suggests Ensign Lovely has marched the length of London, but no further, in procession from Whitehall (what remained of the royal household and Banqueting Hall after a fire in 1698) in the west of London to the Tower of London in the east. The buying of a promotion in the army was a recognized route for preferment. Lovely would undergo a considerable rise from ensign, the lowest rank of officer, to brigadier, in charge of a brigade.

2 An antiquated phrase at the time of the play; a curse, meaning to wish infection or plague on a person.

3 Centlivre conflates Sir James with the popular stage figure Harry Wildair, a gambling rake played by Robert Wilks in George Farquhar's two great successes *The Constant Couple* (1699) and *Sir Harry Wildair* (1701).

bear with the Girl, you deserve her Fortune; here's your Part,[1] (*Gives a Paper*) he'll give you your Cue, he stays at his Lodging for you.

ENSIGN LOVELY. What's the Design?

SIR JAMES COURTLY. That will tell you; quick Dispatch.

ENSIGN LOVELY. Well, Sir *James*, I know you have a Prolifick Brain, and will rely on your Contrivances, and if it succeeds the Captain shall have a Bowl of Punch large enough to set his Ship afloat. (*Exit.*)

Lady Reveller, *Lady* Lucy, *Mrs.* Sago, *appear.*

SIR JAMES COURTLY. The Tea-Table broke up already! I fear there has been but small Recruits of Scandal to Day.

MRS. SAGO. Well, I'll swear I think the Captain's a Pleasant Fellow.

SIR JAMES COURTLY. That's because he made his Court to her. (*Aside.*)

LADY REVELLER. Uh—I Nauseate those Amphibious Creatures.

SIR JAMES COURTLY. Umph, she was not Address'd to.

LADY LUCY. He seems neither to want Sense, Honour, nor True Courage, and methinks there is a Beauty in his Plain Delivery.

SIR JAMES COURTLY. There spoke Sincerity without Affectation.

LADY REVELLER. How shall we pass the Afternoon?

SIR JAMES COURTLY. Aye, Ladies, how shall we?

LADY REVELLER. You here! I thought you had Listed your self Volunteer under the Captain to Board some Prize,[2] you whisper'd so often, and sneak'd out one after another.

SIR JAMES COURTLY. Who would give one self the Pains to Cruise Abroad, when all one Values is at Home?

LADY REVELLER. To whom is this Directed? Or will you Monopolize and Ingross us all?[3]

---

1   An actor's role was separately written out as a "part."

2   Enlisted with the Captain to pursue women.

3   The impact of monopolies on English trade, and the "engrossing" or wholesale purchase of commodities or trading rights, was hotly debated at this time.

SIR JAMES COURTLY. No,—tho' you would wake Desire in every Beholder, I resign you to my Worthy Friend.

LADY LUCY. And the rest of the Company have no Pretence to you.

MRS. SAGO. That's more than she knows. (*Aside.*)

SIR JAMES COURTLY. Beauty, like yours, wou'd give all Mankind Pretence.

MRS. SAGO. So, not a Word to me; are these his Vows? (*In an uneasie Air.*)

LADY LUCY. There's One upon the Teaze already. (*Aside.*)

LADY REVELLER. Why, you are in Disorder, my Dear; you look as if you had lost a *Trant-Leva:*[1] What have you said to her, Sir *James*?

SIR JAMES COURTLY. I said, Madam? I hope I never say any Thing to offend the Ladies. The Devils in these Married Women, they cann't conceal their own Intrigues,† though they Swear us to Secrecy. (*Aside.*)

LADY LUCY. You mistake, Cousin, 'tis his saying nothing to her has put her upon the Fret.

LADY REVELLER. Ay, your Observations are always Malicious.

MRS. SAGO. I despise them, Dear Lady *Reveller*, let's in to Picquet; I suppose Lady *Lucy* would be pleas'd with Sir *James* alone to finish her Remarks.

LADY LUCY. Nay, if you remove the Cause, the Discourse ceases.

SIR JAMES COURTLY. (*Going up to her.*) This you draw upon your self, you will discover it. (*To her.*)

MRS. SAGO. Yes, your Falshood.

LADY REVELLER. Come my Dear, Sir *James*, will you make One at a Pool?[2]

SIR JAMES COURTLY. Pardon me, Madam, I'm to be at *White's* in Half an Hour,[3] anon at the *Basset-Table*. I'm Yours.

MRS. SAGO. No, no, he cann't leave her. (*Going, still looking back.*)

---

1 A term from basset, to gamble for thirty-three times your stake.

2 To become part of a group in a card game.

3 White's Chocolate House in St. James was a Whig meeting place.

LADY LUCY. They play Gold, Sir *James*.

SIR JAMES COURTLY. (*Going up to Lady Lucy*) Madam, were your Heart the Stake I'd Renounce all Engagements to win that, or retrieve my own.

LADY LUCY. I must like the Counterstake very well ere I play so high.

MRS. SAGO. Sir *James*, hearkee, One Word with you. (*Breaking from Lady* Reveller's *Hand, pulling Sir* James *by the Sleeve.*)

LADY LUCY. Ha, ha, I knew she could not stir; I'll remove your Constraint, but, with my wonted Freedom, will tell you plainly—your Husband's Shop wou'd better become you than Gaming and Gallants. Oh Shame to Virtue, that we† shou'd Copy Men in their most Reigning Vices!
Of Virtue's wholesome Rules unjustly we complain,
When Search of Pleasures gives us greater Pain.
How slightly we our Reputation Guard,
Which lost but once can never be Repair'd.

LADY REVELLER. Farewel Sentences.

Enter Alpiew.

ALPIEW. Madam—(*Whispers her Lady.*)

MRS. SAGO. So then, you'd persuade me 'twas the Care of my Fame.

SIR HARRY.[1] Nothing else I protest, my Dear Little Rogue; I have as much Love as you, but I have more Conduct.

MRS. SAGO. Well, you know how soon I forgive you your Faults.

SIR JAMES COURTLY. Now to what Purpose have I Lied my self into her good Graces, when I would be glad to be rid of her? (*Aside.*)

LADY REVELLER. Booted and Spurr'd say you? Pray send him up, Sir *James*; I suppose Trusty *Buckle* is come with some Diverting Embassy from your Friend.

---

1   Once again Sir James is called Sir Harry, in an intertextual slip which reminds the reader of Sir Harry Wildair; see page 80, note 3 above.

Enter Buckle *in a Riding Dress.*

LADY REVELLER.† Why in this Equipage?

BUCKLE. Ah! Madam.—

LADY REVELLER. Out with it.

BUCKLE. Farewell Friends, Parents, and my Country; thou Dear Play-house, and sweet Park, Farewell.

LADY REVELLER. Farewel, why, whither are you going?

BUCKLE. My Lord and I am going where they never knew Deceit.

SIR JAMES COURTLY. That Land is Invisible, *Buckle.*

LADY REVELLER. Ha, ha, ha.

SIR JAMES COURTLY. Were my Lord of my Mind your Ladiship should not have had so large a Theme for your Mirth. Your Servant Ladies. (*Exit.*)

LADY REVELLER. Well, but what's your Business?

BUCKLE. My Lord charg'd me in his Name to take his Everlasting Leave of your Ladiship.

LADY REVELLER. Why, where is he a going pray?

BUCKLE. In search of a Country where there is no Women.

MRS. SAGO. Oh dear, why what have the Women done to him pray?

BUCKLE. Done to him, Madam? He says they are Proud, Perfidious, Vain, Inconstant, Coquets in *England.*

MRS. SAGO. Oh! He'll find they are everywhere the same.

LADY REVELLER. And this is the Cause of his Whimsical Pilgrimage? Ha, ha.

BUCKLE. And this proceeds from your ill Usage, Madam; when he left your House,—he flung himself into his Coach with such a Force, that he broke all the Windows,—as they say,— for my Part I was not there;—when he came Home he beat all his Servants round to be Reveng'd.

ALPIEW. Was you there, *Buckle?*

BUCKLE. No, I thank my Stars, when I arriv'd the Expedition was over;—in Haste he Mounted his Chamber;—flung himself upon his Bed,—Bursting out into a Violent Passion,—Oh that ever I should suffer my self to be impos'd upon, said he, by this Coquetish Beauty!

LADY REVELLER. Meaning me, *Buckle*, Ha, ha?

BUCKLE. Stay till I have finish'd the Piece, Madam, and your Ladiship shall judge;—she's Fickle as she's Fair,—she does not use more Art to Gain a Lover, said he, than to deceive him when he is fix'd.—Humph. (*Leering at her.*)

LADY REVELLER. Pleasant—and does he call this taking Leave?

MRS. SAGO. A Comical Adieu.

BUCKLE. Oh, Madam, I'm not come to the Tragical Part of it yet, starting from his Bed.—

LADY REVELLER. I thought it had been all Farce,—if there be any Thing Heroick in't I'll set my Face and look Grave.

BUCKLE. My Relation will require it, Madam, for I am ready to weep at the Repetition: Had you but seen how often he Travast the Room, (*Acting it*) heard how often he stamp'd, what distort'd Faces he made, casting up his Eyes thus, Biting his Thumbs thus.

LADY REVELLER. Ha, ha, ha, you'll make an Admirable Actor,—shall I speak to the Patentees[1] for you?

MRS. SAGO. But pray how did this end?

BUCKLE. At last, Madam, quite spent with Rage, he sunk down upon his Elbow, and his Head fell upon his Arm.

LADY REVELLER. What, did he faint away?

BUCKLE. Oh, no.

MRS. SAGO. He did not die?

BUCKLE. No, Madam, but he fell asleep.

LADY REVELLER. Oh Brave Prince *Prettiman.*[2]

OMNES. Ha, ha, ha.

BUCKLE. After Three Hours Nap he Wak'd—and calling hastily—my Dear *Buckle*, said he, let's to the End of the World; and try to find a Place where the Sun Shines not here and there at one Time—for 'tis not fit that it should at once look

---

1   The theatre managers. Technically Drury Lane, where *The Basset Table* was performed, under the management of Christopher Rich, was the only theatre holding royal patents from the Crown at this time.

2   Prince Pretty-man is the absurd heroic figure mocked in the Duke of Buckingham's *The Rehearsal* (1671). In Bayes's terrible play-within-a-play the Prince sees his love Cloris and, overcome with emotion ("I am so surpris'd with sleep, I cannot speak the rest"), immediately falls asleep.

upon Two Persons whose Sentiments are so Different—She no longer regards my Pain, Ungrateful, False, Inhumane, Barbarous Woman.

LADY REVELLER. Foolish, Fond, Believing, Easie Man; there's my Answer—Come, shall we to *Picquet*, my Dear?

BUCKLE. Hold, hold, Madam, I han't half done—

MRS. SAGO. Oh! Pray my Dear Lady *Reveller*, let's have it out, 'tis very Diverting—

BUCKLE. He call'd me in a feeble Voice; *Buckle*, said he, bring me my little *Scrutore*[1]— for I will write to Lady *Reveller* before I part from this Place, never to behold her more—what, don't you Cry, Madam?

LADY REVELLER. Cry—No, no, go on, go on.

BUCKLE. 'Tis done, Madam—and there's the Letter. (*Gives her a Letter.*)

LADY REVELLER. So, this Compleats the Narration. (*Reads.*) Madam, *Since I cannot Live in a Place where there is a Possibility of seeing you without Admiring, I resolve to Fly; I am going for* Flanders; *since you are False I have no Business here—I need not describe the Pain I feel, you are but too well Acquainted with that—therefore I'll chuse Death rather than Return.*—Adieu.

BUCKLE. Can any Man in the World write more Tenderly, Madam? Does he not say 'tis Impossible to Love you, and go for *Flanders*? And that he would rather hear of your Death than Return.—

LADY REVELLER. Excellent, Ha, ha.

BUCKLE. What, do you Laugh?

MRS. SAGO. Who can forbear?

BUCKLE. I think you ought to Die with Grief; I warrant Heaven will punish you all. (*Going.*)

ALPIEW. But hearkee, *Buckle*, where are you going now?

BUCKLE. To tell my Lord in what Manner your Lady receiv'd his Letter; Farewel—now for *Flanders*.[2]—

---

1 Writing case.

2 The War of the Spanish Succession, which sought to limit French expansion, resist the French claim to the Spanish throne, and to safeguard Protestant Europe, was fought in Spain and west Europe. Early battles were centred in Flanders, part of the French-held southern Spanish Netherlands, in order to prevent French expansion north into the Protestant United Provinces.

ALPIEW. A fair Wind, and a good Voyage to you. (*As he goes out enter Lord* Worthy.)

BUCKLE. My Lord here? So now may I have my Head Broke for my long Harangue if it comes out.

LADY REVELLER. Oh! Miraculous—my Lord, you have not finish'd your Campaign already, have you? Ha, ha, ha; or has the *French* made Peace hearing of your Lordship's intended Bravery, and left you no Enemies to Combat?†

LORD WORTHY. My worst of Foes are here—here, within my Breast; your Image, Madam.

LADY REVELLER. Oh Dear, my Lord, no more of that Theme, for *Buckle* has given us a Surfeit on't already—even from your Breaking the Glasses of your Coach—to your falling fast Asleep. Ha, ha, ha.

LORD WORTHY. The Glasses of my Coach! What do you mean, Madam—Oh Hell! (*Biting his Thumbs.*)

BUCKLE. Ruined quite—Madam, for Heaven's sake what does your Ladiship Mean? I Li'd in every Syllable I told you, Madam.

LADY REVELLER. Nay, if your Lordship has a Mind to Act it over agen we will Oblige you for once—*Alpiew* set Chairs—come, Dear *Sago*, sit down—and let the Play begin—*Buckle* knows his Part, and upon Necessity cou'd Act yours too my Lord.

LORD WORTHY. What has this Dog been doing? When he was only to deliver my Letter, to give her new Subject for her Mirth—Death, methinks I hate her,—Oh that I cou'd hold that Mind—what makes you in this Equipage? Ha, Sirrah? (*Aside.*)

BUCKLE. My Lord, I, I, I, I,

LORD WORTHY. Peace Villain—(*Strikes him.*)

LADY REVELLER. Hey—this is Changing the Scene—

BUCKLE. Who the Devil would Rack his Brains for these People of Quality, who like no Body's Wit but their own?—(*Aside.*)

MRS. SAGO. If the Beating were Invention before, thou hast it now in Reality; if Wars begin I'll Retire. They may agree better alone perhaps. (*Exit.*)

LADY REVELLER. Where did you learn this Rudeness, my Lord, to Strike your Servant before me?

LORD WORTHY. When you have depriv'd a Man of his Reason how can you blame his Conduct?

BUCKLE. Reason—Egad—there's not Three Drams of Reason between you both—as my Cheek can testifie. (*Aside.*)

LADY REVELLER. The Affront was meant to me—nor will I endure these Passions—I thought I had forbid your Visits.

LORD WORTHY. I thought I had Resolv'd against them too.

ALPIEW. But Resolutions are of small force of either side. (*Aside.*)

LORD WORTHY. Grant me but this One Request and I'll remove this hated Object.

LADY REVELLER. Upon Condition 'tis the last.

LORD WORTHY. It shall—I think it shall at least—Is there a Happy Man for whom I am Despised?

LADY REVELLER. I thought 'twas some such ridiculous Question; I'm of the *Low-Church,* my Lord, consequently hate Confessors; ha, ha, ha.

BUCKLE. And Penance too† I dare Swear. (*Aside.*)

LORD WORTHY. And every thing but Play.

LADY REVELLER. Dare you, the Subject of my Power—you, that Petition Love, Arraign my Pleasures? Now I'm fixt—and will never see you more.

BUCKLE. Now wou'd any Body Swear she's in Earnest.

LORD WORTHY. I cannot bear that Curse—see me at your Feet again, (*Kneels*) Oh! you have Tortur'd me enough, take Pity now Dear Tyrant, and let my Suffering end.

LADY REVELLER. I must not be Friends with him, for then I shall have him at my Elbow all Night, and spoil my Luck at the *Basset-Table.* (*Aside.*) Either Cringing or Correcting, always in Extreams—I am weary of this Fatigue.

He that wou'd gain my Heart must Learn the Way
Not to Controul, but readily to Obey.
For he that once Pretends my Faults to see,
That Moment makes himself all Faults to me. (*Exit.*)

BUCKLE. There's the Inside of a Woman. (*Aside.*)

LORD WORTHY. Gon—now Curses on me for a Fool—the worst of Fools—a Woman's Fool—

Whose only Pleasure is to feed her Pride,
Fond of her Self, she cares for none beside.
So true Coquets on their numerous Charms Display,
And strive to Conquer on purpose to betray.

ACT IV†

Enter Lord Worthy *and Sir* James.

SIR JAMES COURTLY. Well, my Lord. I have left my Cards in
the Hand of a Friend to hear what you have to say to me. Love
I'm sure is the Text, therefore Divide and Subdivide as quick
as you can.

LORD WORTHY. Could'st thou Infuse into me thy Temper, Sir
James, I shou'd have thy Reason too; but I am Born to Love
this Fickle, Faithless Fair—what have I not Essay'd to Race
her from my Breast?[1] But all in Vain; I must have her, or I
must not Live.

SIR JAMES COURTLY. Nay, if you are so far gone, my Lord,
your Distemper requires an Able Physician—what think you
of *Lovely's* bringing a File of Muscqueteers, and carry her
away, *Via & Armis*?[2]

LORD WORTHY. That Way might give her Person to my Arms,
but where's the Heart?

SIR JAMES COURTLY. A Trifle in Competition with her Body.

LORD WORTHY. The Heart's a Gem that I prefer.

SIR JAMES COURTLY. Say you so my Lord? I'll Engage
Three Parts of Europe will make that Exchange with you;
Ha, ha, ha.

LORD WORTHY. That Maxim wou'd hold with me perhaps in
all but her, there I must have both or none; therefore Instruct
me Friend, thou who negligent in Love, keeps always on the
Level with the Fair—what Method shou'd I take to Sound
her Soul's Design? For tho' her Carriage puts me on the Rack
when I behold that Train of Fools about her, yet my Heart will
plead in her Excuse, and Calm my Anger Spite of all Efforts.

---

1   An excessively poetic way to say "What have I not tried to erase her from my heart."

2   A unit of soldiers armed with muskets. "Vi et armis" Latin for by force of arms, by
compulsion.

SIR JAMES COURTLY. Humph? I have a Plot, my Lord, if you'll comply with it.

LORD WORTHY. Nothing of Force.

SIR JAMES COURTLY. Whate're it be you shall be Witness of it, 'twill either Quench your Flame, or Kindle hers. I only will appear the Guilty; but here's Company, I'll tell you all within.

Enter Captain *and* Lovely *Drest like a Tar.*[1]

LORD WORTHY. I'll expect you. (*Exit.*)

SIR JAMES COURTLY. Ha, Captain, How sits the Wind between you and your Mistress? Ha?

CAPTAIN HEARTY. North and by South, Faith; but here's one Sails full East, and without some unexpected Tornado, from the Old Man's Coast—he makes his Port I warrant ye.

ENSIGN LOVELY. I wish I were at Anchor once.

SIR JAMES COURTLY. Why, thou art as arrant a Tar as if thou hadst made an *East-India V*oyage, ha, ha.[2]

ENSIGN LOVELY. Ay, am I not, Sir *James*? But Egad I hope the Old Fellow understands nothing of Navigation; if he does I shall be at a loss for the Terms.

SIR JAMES COURTLY. Oh! no matter for Terms—look big, and Bluster for your Country—describe the *Vigo* Business[3]— publick News will furnish you with that, and I'll engage the Success.

CAPTAIN HEARTY. Ay, Ay, let me alone, I'll bear up with Sir *Richard*, and thou shalt Board his Pinnace[4] with Consent ne'er fear—ho, here he comes full Sail.

---

1 A sailor.

2 The united East India Company, after 1702, was one of the largest trading concerns in Britain. Trade with India accounted for a large proportion of Britain's imports, and voyages were regular.

3 The naval battle of Vigo (1702) in north-west Spain was one of the opening skirmishes of the War of the Spanish Succession. Much of a Spanish treasure fleet was taken from French protection. This was a welcome success after the ignominious failure of the Anglo-Dutch siege of Cadiz.

4 A small two-masted vessel, frequently used as a metaphor for a woman, or mistress, here Valeria.

Enter Sir Richard.

Sir *Richard.* I'm glad to see you; this is my Kinsman which I told you of, as soon as he Landed; I brought him to Kiss your Hands.

SIR RICHARD PLAINMAN. I Honour you, you are welcome.

ENSIGN LOVELY. I thank you Sir,—I'm not for Compliments; 'tis a Land Language I understand it not; Courage, Honesty, and Plain-dealing Truth, is the Learning of our Element; if you like that I am for ye.

SIR JAMES COURTLY. (*Aside to the Captain.*) The Rogue does it to a Miracle.

CAPTAIN HEARTY. He's an improving Spark I find, ha, ha.

SIR RICHARD PLAINMAN.† Like it, Sir, why 'tis the only Thing I do like, hang Compliments, and Court-Breeding, it serves only to make Men a Prey to one another, to Encourage Cowardice, and Ruin Trade—No, Sir, give me the Man that dares meet Death and Dinner with the same Appetite—one who rather than let in Popery, wou'd let out his Blood; to Maintain such Men I'd pay Double Custom; nay, all my Gain shou'd go for their Support.

SIR JAMES COURTLY. The best Well-wisher to his Country of an *Englishman* I ever heard.

ENSIGN LOVELY. Oh, Sir *Richard*, I wish the Nation were all of your Mind, 'twould give the Soldiers and the Sailors Life. Captain launch off a round Lie or Two.†[1]

CAPTAIN HEARTY. And make us Fight with Heart and Hand; my Kinsman, I'll assure you, fits your Principle to a Hair; He hates the *French* so much he ne'er fails to give them a Broadside where'er he meets them; and has Brought in more Privateers[2] this War than half the Captains in the *Navy*; he was the first Man that Boarded the *French Fleet* at *Vigo*—and in *Gibraltar*

---

1 "Captain launch off a round Lie or Two (*Aside to Ensign*)" is a mis-transposed line, corrected to this setting in D1 and 1735 editions, but probably intended for Sir James Courtly immediately after Sir Richard's previous speech.

2 Private mercenary vessels, under government commission, that specialized in attack on merchant vessels.

Business[1]—the *Gazettes*[2] will inform you of the Name of Captain *Match*.

SIR JAMES COURTLY. Is this that Captain *Match*?

ENSIGN LOVELY. For want of better, Sir.

SIR JAMES COURTLY. Sir, I shall be Proud of being known to you.

SIR RICHARD PLAINMAN. And I of being Related to you, Sir—I have a Daughter Young and Handsome, and I'll give her a Portion shall make thee an Admiral Boy; for a Soul like thine is fit only to Command a Navy—what say'st thou, art thou for a Wife?

SIR JAMES COURTLY. So, 'tis done, ha, ha, ha. (*Aside.*)

CAPTAIN HEARTY. A prosperous Gale I'faith.

ENSIGN LOVELY. I don't know, Sir *Richard*, mehap a Woman may not like me; I am Rough and Storm-like in my Temper, unacquainted with the Effeminacy of Courts; I was Born upon the Sea, and since I can remember never Liv'd Two Months on Shore; if I Marry my Wife must go Abroad, I promise you that.

SIR RICHARD PLAINMAN. Abroad Man? Why she shall go to the *Indies* with thee—Oh! such a Son-in-Law—how shall I be Blest in My Posterity? Now do I foresee the Greatness of my Grand-Children; the Sons of this Man shall, in the Age to come, make *France* a Tributary Nation.

ENSIGN LOVELY. Once in an Engagement, Sir, as I was giving Orders to my Men, comes a Ball and took off a Fellow's Head, and struck it full in my Teeth; I wipp'd it up, clapp'd it into a Gun, and shot it at the Enemy again.

SIR RICHARD PLAINMAN. Without the least Concern?

ENSIGN LOVELY. Concern, Sir,—ha, ha, ha, if it had been my own Head I would have done the like.

SIR RICHARD PLAINMAN. Prodigious Effect of Courage!— Captain I'll fetch my Girl, and be here again in an Instant:— What an Honour 'twill be to have such a Son! (*Exit.*)

---

1   The English captured Gibraltar from the Spanish in 1704.

2   The Gazettes were official government newspapers, printed in London, Dublin, and Edinburgh.

CAPTAIN HEARTY. Ha, ha, ha, ha, you outdo your Master.

SIR JAMES COURTLY. Ha, ha, ha, ha, the Old Knight's Transported.

ENSIGN LOVELY. I wish 'twas over, I am all in a Sweat; here he comes again.

Enter Sir Richard *and* Valeria.

SIR RICHARD PLAINMAN. I'll hear none of your Excuses,—Captain your Hand,—there take her,—and these Gentlemen shall be Witnesses, if they please, to this Paper, wherein I give her my whole Estate when I die, and Twenty Thousand Pounds down upon the Nail; I care not whether my Boy be worth a Groat,—get me but Grandsons and I'm Rich enough.

CAPTAIN HEARTY. Generously said I'faith—much Good may do him with her.

ENSIGN LOVELY. I'll do my Endeavour,† Father, I promise you.

SIR JAMES COURTLY. I wish you Joy, Captain and you, Madam.

VALERIA. That's Impossible;—can I have Joy in a Species so very different from my own? Oh my Dear *Lovely*!—We were only form'd one for another;—thy Dear Enquiring Soul is more to me—than all these useless Lumps of Animated Clay: Duty compels my Hand,—but my Heart is subject only to my Mind,—the Strength of that they cannot Conquer;—no, with the Resolution of the Great Unparallell'd *Epictetus*,[1]—I here protest my Will shall ne're assent to any but my *Lovely*.

SIR RICHARD PLAINMAN. Ay, you and your Will may Philosophize as long as you please,—Mistress,—but your Body shall be taught another Doctrine,—it shall so,—Your Mind,—and your Soul, quotha! Why, what a Pox has my Estate to do with them? Ha? 'Tis the Flesh Huswife, that must raise Heirs,—and Supporters of my Name;—and since I knew the getting of the Estate, 'tis fit I shou'd dispose of it,—and therefore no more Excuses, this is your Husband do you see,—take my Word for it.

---

1   Epictetus (ca. 55-135) was a Stoic philosopher who taught that a philosophical life of reason, free from the passions, brought happiness.

VALERIA.

> *The outward empty Form of Marriage take*
> *But all beyond I keep for* Lovely's *Sake.*
> *Thus on the Ground for ever fix my Eyes;*
> *All Sights but* Lovely *shall their Balls despise.*

SIR RICHARD PLAINMAN. Come, Captain,—my Chaplain is within, he shall do the Business this Minute: If I don't use the Authority of a Father, this Baggage will make me lose such a Son-in-Law that the City's Wealth cann't purchase me his Fellow. (*Aside.*)

ENSIGN LOVELY.

> *Thanks Dear Invention for this Timely Aid.*
> *The Bait's gone†down, he's by himself betray'd.*
> *Thus still where Art both True and Honest fail,*
> *Deceitful Wit and Policy prevail.*

VALERIA. To Death, or any Thing,—'tis all alike to me. (*Exit cum Valeria.*)

SIR RICHARD PLAINMAN. Get you in I say,—Hussey, get you in. In my Conscience my Niece has spoil'd her already; but I'll have her Married this Moment; Captain, you have bound me ever to you by this Match, command me and my House for ever.—But shall I not have your Company, Gentlemen, to be Witnesses of this Knot, this joyful Knot?

CAPTAIN HEARTY. Yes Faith, Sir *Richard*, I have too much Respect for my Kinsman to leave him—till I see him safe in Harbour; I'll wait upon you presently.

SIR JAMES COURTLY. I am engag'd in the next Room at Play, I beg your Pardon, Sir *Richard*, for an Hour; I'll bring the whole Company to Congratulate the Bride and Bridegroom.

SIR RICHARD PLAINMAN. Bride and Bridegroom? Congratulate me, Man: Methinks I already see my Race Recorded amongst the foremost Heroes of my Nation.—Boys, all Boys, and all Soldiers.

> *They shall the Pride of* France *and* Spain *pull down,*
> *And add their* Indies *to our* English *Crown.* (*Exit.*)

SIR JAMES COURTLY. Ha, ha, ha, never was Man so Bigotted before;—how will this end when he discovers the Cheat? Ha, ha, won't you make One with the Ladies, Captain?

CAPTAIN HEARTY. I don't care if I do venture a Piece or Two,

I'll but dispatch a little Business and meet you at the Table, Sir *James*. (*Exit.*)

Enter Lady Lucy.

SIR JAMES COURTLY. Ha, Lady *Lucy*! Is your Ladiship reconcil'd to *Basset* yet? Will you give me leave to lose this Purse to you, Madam?

LADY LUCY. I thank Fortune I neither wish, nor need it, Sir *James*; I presume the next Room is furnish'd with Avarice enough to serve you in that Affair, if it is a Burden to you; or Mrs. *Sago's* ill Luck may give you an Opportunity of returning some of the Obligations you lye under.

SIR JAMES COURTLY. Your Sex, Madam, extorts a Duty from ours, and a well-bred Man can no more refuse his Money to a Lady, than his Sword to a Friend.

LADY LUCY. That Superfluity of good Manners, Sir *James*, would do better Converted into Charity; this Town abounds with Objects—wou'd it not leave a more Glorious Fame behind you to be the Founder of some Pious Work; when all the Poor at mention of your Name shall Bless your Memory; than that Posterity shou'd say you Wasted your Estate on Cards and Women?

SIR JAMES COURTLY. Humph, 'tis pity she were not a Man, she Preaches so Emphatically. (*Aside.*) Faith, Madam, you have a very good Notion, but something too Early—when I am Old, I may put your Principles in Practice, but Youth for Pleasure was design'd—

LADY LUCY. The truest Pleasure must consist in doing Good, which cannot be in Gaming.

SIR JAMES COURTLY. Every thing is good in its Kind, Madam; Cards are harmless Bits of Paper, Dice insipid Bones—and Women made for Men.

LADY LUCY. Right, Sir *James*—but all these things may be perverted—Cards are harmless Bits of Paper in themselves, yet through them what Mischiefs have been Done? What Orphans Wrong'd? What Tradesmen Ruin'd? What Coach and Equipage[1] dismist for them?

---

1 Attendant servants for a carriage.

SIR JAMES COURTLY. But then, how many fine Coaches and Equipages have they set up, Madam?

LADY LUCY. Is it the more Honourable for that? How many Misses[1] keep Coaches too? Which Arrogance in my Opinion only makes them more Eminently Scandalous—

SIR JAMES COURTLY. Oh! those are such, as have a Mind to be Damn'd in this State, Madam—but I hope your Ladiships don't Rank them amongst us Gamesters.

LADY LUCY. They are Inseparable, Sir James; Madam's Grandeur must be Upheld—tho' the Baker and Butcher shut up Shop.

SIR JAMES COURTLY. Oh! your Ladiship wrongs us middling Gentlemen there; to Ruin Tradesmen is the Qualities Prerogative only; and none beneath a Lord can pretend to do't with an Honourable Air, ha, ha.

LADY LUCY. Their Example sways the meaner Sort; I grieve to think that Fortune shou'd Exalt such Vain, such Vicious† Souls—whilst Virtue's Cloath'd in Raggs.

SIR JAMES COURTLY. Ah! Faith, she'd make but a scurvy Figure at Court, Madam, the States-men and Politicians wou'd Suppress her quickly—but whilst she remains in your Breast she's safe—and makes us all in Love with that Fair Covering.

LADY LUCY. Oh! Fie, Fi, Sir James, you cou'd not Love one that hates your chief Direction.

SIR JAMES COURTLY. I shou'd Hate it too, Madam, on some Terms† I coul'd Name.

LADY LUCY. What wou'd make that Conversion pray?

SIR JAMES COURTLY. Your Heart.

LADY LUCY. I cou'd pay that Price—but dare not Venture on one so Wild—(*Aside.*) First let me see the Fruit e'er I take a Lease of the Garden, Sir James.

SIR JAMES COURTLY. Oh! Madam, the best Way is to Secure the Ground, and then you may Manure and Cultivate it as you please.

LADY LUCY. That's a certain Trouble and uncertain Profit, and in this Affair; I prefer the Theory before the Practick. But I detain you from the Table, Sir James—you are wanted to

---

1 Kept mistresses.

Tally[1]—your Servant—(*Exit.*)

SIR JAMES COURTLY. Nay, if you leave me, Madam, the Devil will Tempt me—she's gone, and now cann't I shake off the Thought of Seven Wins, Eight Loses—for the Blood of me—and all this Grave Advice of hers is lost, Faith—tho' I do Love her above the rest of her Sex—she's an exact Model of what all Women ought to be,—and yet your Merry little Coquettish Tits[2] are very Diverting—well, now for *Basset*; let me see what Money I have about—me, Humph, about a Hundred *Guineas*—half of which will set the Ladies to Cheating—false Parolies[3] in Abundance.
Each Trifling toy wou'd Tempt in Times of Old,
Now nothing Melts a Woman's Heart like Gold.
Some Bargains Drive, other's more Nice then they,
Who'd have you think they Scorn to Kiss for Pay;
To Purchase them you must Lose Deep at Play.
With several Women, several Ways Prevail;
But Gold's a certain Way that cannot Fail. (*Exit.*)

The Scene Draws, and Discovers Lady Reveller, *Mrs.* Sago, *and several Gentlemen and Ladies round a Table at* Basset.

Enter Sir James.

LADY REVELLER. Oh! Sir *James*, are you come? We want you to Tally for us.

SIR JAMES COURTLY. What Luck, Ladies?

LADY REVELLER. I have only won a *Sept & Leva*.[4]

MRS. SAGO. And I have lost a *Trante & Leva*[5]—my Ill Fortune has not forsook me yet I see.

SIR JAMES COURTLY. I go a *Guinea* upon that Card.[6]

LADY REVELLER. You lose that Card.

---

1 To deal at basset, to play the role of banker.

2 Young women, "usually in depreciation or disapproval: esp. one of loose character, a hussy" (*OED*).

3 A term from basset, to turn up the corner of a winning card to increase your stake.

4 To win twice on the same card, and take seven times your stake.

5 To win four times on the same card and take thirty-three times your stake.

6 Charles Cotton's description of basset (Appendix B1) suggests players only bet on their own cards, but here the players also bet on the fortunes of each other's cards.

MRS. SAGO. I Mace[1] Sir *James's* Card Double.

BANKER. Seven wins, and Five loses; you have lost it, Madam.

MRS. SAGO. Agen?—sure never was Woman so Unlucky—

BANKER. Knave wins, and Ten loses; you have Won, Sir *James.*

LADY REVELLER. Clean Cards here.

MRS. SAGO. Burn this Book,[2] 't has an unlucky† Air. (*Tears them.*) Bring some more Books.

Enter Captain.

LADY REVELLER. Oh! Captain—here set a Chair, come, Captain, you shall sit by me—now if we can but Strip this Tarr. (*Aside.*)

CAPTAIN HEARTY. Withal my Heart, Madam—come, what do you Play Gold?—that's something High tho'—well a *Guinea* upon this Honest Knave of Clubs.

LADY REVELLER. You lose it for a *Guinea* more.

CAPTAIN HEARTY. Done, Madam.

BANKER. The Five Wins, and the Knave loses.

LADY REVELLER. You have lost it, Captain.

SIR JAMES COURTLY. The Knave wins, for Two Guineas more, Madam.

LADY REVELLER. Done Sir *James.*

BANKER. Six Wins—Knave, Loses.

SIR JAMES COURTLY. Oh! the Devil, I'm Fac'd,†[3] I had rather have lost it all.

BANKER. Nine wins, Queen loses—you have won.

MRS. SAGO. I'll make a Paroli—I Mace as much more; your Card loses Sir *James,* for Two Guineas, your's Captain, loses for a Guineas more.

BANKER. Four wins, Nine loses—you have Lost, Madam.

MRS. SAGO. Oh! I cou'd Tear my Flesh—as I Tear these Cards—Confusion—I can never win above a wretch'd *Paroli*; for if I

---

1 Technically, Masse, to increase your stake on a winning card.

2 Each player in basset has a "book" of thirteen cards before them.

3 Possibly, beaten by a face card, a court card; or Fasse, the Tallier turns the first card in a new pack and wins money from every card of that kind with a stake on it; see Appendix B1.

push to *Sept & Leva*, 'tis gone. (*Walks about Disorderly.*)

BANKER. Ace wins, Knave loses.

CAPTAIN HEARTY. Sink the Knave, I'll set no more on't.

LADY REVELLER. Fac't† agen—what's the meaning of this Ill-luck to Night? Bring me a Book of Hearts, I'll try if they are more Successful, that on the Queen; yours and your Cards loses.

MRS. SAGO. Bring me a fresh Book; bring me another Book; bring me all Diamonds. (*Looks upon them One by One, then throws them over her Shoulders.*)

LADY REVELLER. That can never be lucky, the Name of *Jewels* don't become a Citizen's Wife. (*Aside.*)

BANKER. King wins, the Tray[1] loses.

SIR JAMES COURTLY. You have great Luck to Night, Mr. *Sharper.*

SHARPER. So I have Sir *James*—I have won *Sonica*[2] every time.

LADY REVELLER. But if he has got the Nack of winning thus he shall sharp no more here, I promise him. (*Aside.*)

MRS. SAGO. I Mace that.

LADY REVELLER. Sir *James*, pray will you Tally.

SIR JAMES COURTLY. With all my Heart, Madam. (*Takes the Cards and shuffles them.*)

MRS. SAGO. Pray give me the Cards, Sir. (*Takes 'em and shuffles 'em, and gives 'em to him again.*)

CAPTAIN HEARTY. I set that.[3]

LADY REVELLER. I set Five Guineas upon this Card, Sir *James.*

SIR JAMES COURTLY. Done Madam,—Five wins,—Six loses.

MRS. SAGO. I Set that.

SIR JAMES COURTLY. Five don't go, and Seven loses.

CAPTAIN HEARTY. I Mace double.

LADY REVELLER. I Mace that.

SIR JAMES COURTLY. Three wins, Six loses.

MRS. SAGO. I Mace, I Mace double, and that—Oh ye malicious

---

1   Version of French "trois," three.

2   Sonica: immediately; see page 49, note 1.

3   Lay down a bet.

Stars!—again.

SIR JAMES COURTLY. Eight wins Seven loses.

CAPTAIN HEARTY. So, this *Trante & leva* makes some Amends;—Adsbud I hate Cheating,—What's that false Cock[1] made for now? Ha, Madam?

LADY REVELLER. Nay, Mrs. *Sago*, if you begin to play foul.

MRS. SAGO. Rude Brute, to take Notice of the Slight of Hand in our Sex—I protest he wrongs me, Madam,—there's the *Dernier*[2] Stake,—and I set it all,—now Fortune Favour me, or this Moment is my last.

LADY REVELLER. There's the last of Fifty Pounds,—what's the meaning of this?

SIR JAMES COURTLY. Now for my Plot, her Stock is low I perceive. (*Slips a Purse of Gold into the Furbeloes of Lady* Reveller's *Apron.*)

LADY REVELLER. I never had such ill Luck,—I must fetch more Money: Ha; from whence comes this? This is the Genteelest Piece of Gallantry, the Action is Sir *Harry's* I see by his Eyes.[3] (*Discovers a Purse in the Furbeloes of her Apron.*)

SIR JAMES COURTLY. Nine wins, Six loses.

MRS. SAGO. I am ruin'd and undone for ever; oh, oh, oh, to lose every Card, oh, oh, oh. (*Burst out a Crying.*)

CAPTAIN HEARTY. So there's one Vessel sprung aleek, and I am almost ashoar—If I go on at this Rate, I shall make but a lame Voyage on't I doubt.

SIR JAMES COURTLY. Duce wins, King loses.

CAPTAIN HEARTY. I Mace again,—I Mace Double, I mace again;—now the Devil blow my Head off if ever I saw Cards run so; Dam 'em. (*Tears the Cards, and stamps on 'em.*)

SIR JAMES COURTLY. Fie, Captain, this Concern among the Ladies is indecent.

CAPTAIN HEARTY. Dam the Ladies,—mayn't I swear,—or

---

1 Mrs. Sago has turned up the corner of a card (a paroli) as if it had won, to increase her winnings from it on the next turn.

2 French, last.

3 Once again, Robert Wilks as Sir James is referred to as Sir Harry, from his success in Farquhar's *Sir Harry Wildair*; see page 80, note 3.

tear my Cards if I please, I'm sure I have paid for them; pray count the Cards, I believe there's is a false Tally.

SIR JAMES COURTLY. No, they are Right, Sir. (*Sir* James *counts em.*)

MRS. SAGO. Not to turn One Card! Oh, oh, oh. (*Stamps up and down.*)

LADY REVELLER. Madam, if you play no longer pray don't disturb those that do.—Come, Courage, Captain,—Sir *James's* Gold was very lucky;—who cou'd endure these Men did they not lose their Money? (*Aside.*)

CAPTAIN HEARTY. Bring another Book here;—that upon Ten,—and I Mace that. (*Puts down a Card, and turns another.*)

SIR JAMES COURTLY. King face't, Eight wins, Ten loses.

CAPTAIN HEARTY. Fire and Gunpowder. (*Exit.*)

LADY REVELLER. Ha, ha, ha, what is the Captain vanish'd in his own Smoak?—Come, I Bett with you, Mr. *Sharper*; your Card loses.

Re-enter Captain, *pulling in a Stranger, which he had fetch'd out of the Street.*

CAPTAIN HEARTY. Sir, do you think it is possible to lose a *Trante & Leva,* a *Quinze-leva,*—and a *Sept-et-leva,*—and never turn once.

STRANGER. No sure, 'tis almost Impossible.

CAPTAIN HEARTY. Ounds you lie, I did Sir. (*Laying his Hand on his Sword.*)

LADY REVELLER *and all the Women.* Ah, ah, ah, ah. (*Shrieks and run off.*)

CAPTAIN HEARTY. What the Devil, had I to do among these Land-Rats?—Zounds, to lose Forty Pounds for nothing, not so much as a Wench for it; Ladies, quotha,—a Man had as good be acquainted with Pick-pockets. (*Exit.*)

SIR JAMES COURTLY. Ha, ha, ha, the Captain has frighted the Women out of their Wits,—now to keep my Promise with my Lord, tho' the Thing has but an ill Face, no Matter.

They join together to Enslave us Men,
And why not we to Conquer them again.

ACT V

Enter Sir James *on one side, and Lady* Reveller *on the other.*

LADY REVELLER. Sir *James*, what have you done with the Rude Porpois?

SIR JAMES COURTLY. He is gone to your Uncle's Apartment, Madam, I suppose.—I was in Pain till I knew how your Ladiship did after your Fright.

LADY REVELLER. Really, Sir *James*, the Fellow has put me into the Spleen by his ill Manners. Oh my Stars! That there should be such an unpolished Piece of Humane Race, to be in that Disorder for losing his Money to us Women.—I was apprehensive he would have beat me, ha, ha.

SIR JAMES COURTLY. Ha, ha, your Ladiship must impute his ill Breeding to the Want of Conversation with your Sex; but he is a Man of Honour with his own, I assure you.

LADY REVELLER. I hate out of fashion'd Honour.—But where's the Company, Sir *James*? Shan't we Play again?

SIR JAMES COURTLY. All disperss'd, Madam.

LADY REVELLER. Come, you and I'll go to Picquet then.

SIR JAMES COURTLY. Oh I'm tir'd with Cards, Madam, cann't you think of some other Diversion to pass a chearful Hour?—I cou'd tell you One if you'd give me leave.

LADY REVELLER. Of your own Invention? Then it must be a pleasant One.

SIR JAMES COURTLY. Oh the pleasantest one in the World.

LADY REVELLER. What is it I pray?

SIR JAMES COURTLY. Love, Love, my Dear Charmer. (*Approaches her.*)

LADY REVELLER. Oh Cupid! How came that in your Head?

SIR JAMES COURTLY. Nay, 'tis in my Heart, and except you pity me the Wound is Mortal.

LADY REVELLER. Ha, ha, ha, is Sir *James* got into my Lord *Worthy's* Class?—You that could tell me I should not have so large a Theme for my Diversion, were you in his Place, ha, ha, ha; what, and is the Gay, the Airy, the Witty, Inconstant, Sir *James* overtaken? Ha, ha.

SIR JAMES COURTLY. Very true, Madam,—you see there is no jesting with Fire.—Will you be kind? (*Gets between her and the Door.*)

LADY REVELLER. Kind? What a dismal Sound was there?— I'm afraid your Feaver's high, Sir *James*, ha, ha.

SIR JAMES COURTLY. If you think so, Madam, 'tis time to apply cooling Medicines. (*Locks the Door.*)

LADY REVELLER. Ha, what Insolence is this? The Door lock'd! What do you mean Sir *James*?

SIR JAMES COURTLY. Oh 'tis something indecent to Name it, Madam, but I intend to show you. (*Lays hold on her.*)

LADY REVELLER. Unhand me, Villain, or I'll cry out—

SIR JAMES COURTLY. Do, and make your self the Jest of Servants, expose your Reputation to their vile Tongues,—which if you please shall remain safe within my Breast; but if with your own Noise you Blast it, here I bid Defiance to all Honour and Secrecy,—the First Man than enters dies. (*Struggles with her.*)

LADY REVELLER. What shall I do? Instruct me Heaven— Monster, is this your Friendship to my Lord? And can you wrong the Woman he Adores.

SIR JAMES COURTLY. Ay, but the Woman does not care a Souse[1] for him; and therefore he has no Right above me; I love you as much, and will possess.

LADY REVELLER. Oh! hold—Kill me rather than destroy my Honour—what Devil has Debauch'd your Temper? Or how has my Carriage drawn this Curse upon me? What have I done to give you cause to think you ever shou'd succeed this hated Way. (*Weeps.*)

SIR JAMES COURTLY. Why this Question, Madam? Can a Lady that loves Play so passionately as you do—that takes as much Pains to draw Men in to lose their Money, as a Town

---

1 French "sou," a very small coin.

Miss to their Destruction—that Caresses all Sorts of People for your Interest, that divides your time between your Toylet and the *Basset-Table*; Can you, I say, boast of Innate Virtue?— Fie, fie, I am sure you must have guess'd for what I Play'd so Deep—we never part with our Money without Design—or writing Fool upon our Foreheads;[1]—therefore no more of this Resistance, except you would have more Money.

LADY REVELLER. Oh! horrid.

SIR JAMES COURTLY. There was Fifty Guineas in that Purse, Madam—here's Fifty more; Money shall be no Dispute. (*Offers her Money.*)

LADY REVELLER. (*Strikes it Down.*) Perish your Money with your self—you Villain—there, there; take your boasted Favours which I resolv'd before to have Repaid in *Specie*;[2] Basest of Men I'll have your Life for this Affront—what ho, within there.

SIR JAMES COURTLY. Hush—Faith, you'll Raise the House. (*Lays hold on her.*) And 'tis in Vain—you are mine; nor will I quit this Room till I'm Possest. (*Struggles.*)

LADY REVELLER. Raise the House, I'll raise the World in my Defence, help, Murther, Murther,—a Rape, a Rape—

Enter Lord Worthy *from another Room with his Sword Drawn.*

LORD WORTHY. Ha! Villain, unhand the Lady—or this Moment is thy last.

SIR JAMES COURTLY. Villain, Back my Lord—follow me. (*Exit.*)

LADY REVELLER. By the Bright Sun that Shines you shall not go—no, you have sav'd my Virtue, and I will preserve your Life—let the vile Wretch be punish'd by viler Hands—yours shall not be Prophan'd with Blood so Base, if I have any Power—

LORD WORTHY. Shall the Traytor Live?—Tho' your Barbarous Usage does not Merit this from me, yet in Consideration that I Lov'd you once—I will Chastise his Insolence.

---

1 "Unless we are obvious fools"; also an allusion to cuckolding, where a cuckolded fool is said to wear horns on his forehead.

2 Latin, in kind.

LADY REVELLER. Once—Oh! say not once; do you not Love me still? Oh! how pure your Soul appears to me above that Detested Wretch. (*Weeps.*)

SIR JAMES COURTLY. (*Peeping.*) It takes as I cou'd Wish—

LORD WORTHY. Yet how have I been slighted, every Fop preferr'd to me?—Now you Discover what Inconveniency your Gaming has brought you into—this from me wou'd have been unpardonable Advice—now you have prov'd it at your own Expence.

LADY REVELLER. I have, and hate my self for all my Folly— Oh! forgive me—and if still you think me Worthy of your Heart—I here Return you Mine—and will this Hour Sign it with my Hand.

SIR JAMES COURTLY. How I Applaud my self for this Contrivance.

LORD WORTHY. Oh! the Transporting Joy, it is the only Happiness I Covet here.
Haste then my Charmer, haste the long'd-for Bliss.
The only Happy Minutes of my Life is this. (*Exit.*)

SIR JAMES COURTLY. Ha, ha, ha, ha, how I am Censur'd now for doing this Lady a Piece† of Service, in forcing that upon her, which only her Vanity and Pride Restrain'd.
So Blushing Maids refuse the Court'd Joy,
Tho' wishing Eys—and pressing Hands Comply,
Till by some Stratagem the Lover Gains,
What she deny'd to all his Amorous Pains.

As Sir James is going off, enter Lady Lucy meeting him.

SIR JAMES COURTLY. Ha, Lady *Lucy*!—Having Succeeded for my Friend, who knows but this may be my Lucky Minute too?—Madam, you come Opportunely to hear. (*Takes her by the Hand.*)

LADY LUCY. Stand off Basest of Men, I have heard too much; coud'st thou Chuse no House but this to Act thy Villanies in? And cou'd'st thou fairly offer Vows to me, when thy Heart, Poison'd by vicious Thoughts, harbour'd these Designs against my Family?

SIR JAMES COURTLY. Very fine, Faith, this is like to be my Lucky Minute with a Witness; but Madam—

LADY LUCY. Offer not at Excuses, 'tis height of Impudence to look me in the Face.

SIR JAMES COURTLY. Egad she Loves me—Oh! Happy Rogue—this Concern can proceed from nothing else. (*Aside*.)

LADY LUCY. My Heart till now unus'd to Passion swells with this Affront, wou'd Reproach thee—wou'd Reproach my self, for having Harbour'd one favourable Thought of thee.

SIR JAMES COURTLY. Why did you, Madam?—Egad I owe more to her Anger than ever I did to her Morals.

LADY LUCY. Ha! What have I said?

SIR JAMES COURTLY. The only kind Word you ever utter'd.

LADY LUCY. Yes, Imposture, know to thy Confusion that I did love thee,† and fancy'd I Discover'd some Seeds of Virtue amongst that Heap of Wickedness; but this last Action has betray'd the Fond Mistake, and show'd thou art all o'er Feign'd.

SIR JAMES COURTLY. Give me leave, Madam—

LADY LUCY. Think not this Confession meant to advance thy Impious Love, but hear my Final Resolution.

SIR JAMES COURTLY. Egad I must hear it—I find for there's no stopping her.

LADY LUCY. From this Moment I'll never—

SIR JAMES COURTLY. (*Clapping his Hand before Her Mouth.*) Nay, nay, nay, after Sentence no Criminal is allow'd to Plead; therefore I will be heard—not Guilty, not Guilty. Madam, by—if I don't prove that this is all a Stratagem, Contriv'd, Study'd, Design'd, Prosecut'd, and put in Execution, to reclaim your Cousin, and give my Lord Possession—may you Finish your Curse, and I Doom'd to Everlasting Absence—Egad I'm out of Breath—

LADY LUCY. Oh! Coud'st thou prove this?

SIR JAMES COURTLY. I can, if by the Proof you'll make me Happy; my Lord shall Convince you.

LADY LUCY. To him I will refer it, on this Truth your Hopes Depend.

In Vain we strive our Passions to Conceal,
Our very Passions does our Loves Reveal;

When once the Heart, yields to the Tyrants Sway,
The Eyes or Tongue will soon the Flame Betray. (Exit.)
SIR JAMES COURTLY. I was never out at a Critical Minute in
my Life.

Enter Mr. Sago *and Two Baliffs meeting* Alpiew.

MR. SAGO.† Heakee, Mistress, is my Wife here?

ALPIEW. Truly I shant give my self the Trouble of seeking her
for him; now she has lost all her Money—your Wife is a very
Indiscreet Person, Sir.

MR. SAGO. I'm afraid I shall find it to my Cost.

BALIFFS. Come, come, Sir, we cann't wait all Day—the Actions
are a Thousand Pound—you shall have time to send for Bail,
and what Friends you Please.

MR. SAGO. A Thousand Pound? (*Enter Mrs.* Sago.) Oh! Lambkin
have you Spent me a Thousand Pound.

MRS. SAGO. Who, I Pudd? Oh! undone for Ever—

MR. SAGO. Pud me no Pud,—do you Owe Mr. *Tabby* the *Mercer*
Two Hundred Pounds? Ha.

MRS. SAGO. I, I, I, don't know the Sum Dear Pudd—but, but,
but I do Owe him something; but I believe he made me Pay
too Dear.

MR. SAGO. Oh! thou Wolfkin instead of Lambkin—for thou
hast Devour'd my Substance; and dost thou Owe Mr. *Dollor*
the *Goldsmith* Three Hundred Pound? Dost thou? Ha, speak
Tygress.

MRS. SAGO. Sure it cann't be quite Three Hundred Pound.
(*Sobbing.*)

MR. SAGO. Thou *Island* Crocodile thou—and dost thou Owe
Ratsbane the *Vintner* a Hundred Pound? and were those
Hampers of Wine which I receiv'd so Joyfully sent by thy self,
to thy self? Ha.

MRS. SAGO. Yes indeed, Puddy—I, I, I, beg your Pardon. (*Sobbing.*)

MR. SAGO. And why didst not thou tell me of them? Thou
Rattle-snake—for they say they have sent a Hundred times
for their Money—else I had not been Arrested in my
Shop.

MRS. SAGO. Be, be, be, because I, I, I was afraid, Dear Puddy. (*Crying.*)

MR. SAGO. But wer't not thou afraid to Ruin me tho, Dear Pudd. Ah! I need ask thee, no more Questions, thou Serpent in Petticoats; did I Doat upon thee for this? Here's a Bill from *Calico* the *Linnen-Draper*, another from *Setwell* the *Jeweller*—from *Coupler* a *Mantua-Maker*, and *Pimpwell* the *Milliner*; a Tribe of Locusts enough to undo a Lord Mayor.

MRS. SAGO. I hope not, truly, Dear, Dearey, I'm sure that's all.

MR. SAGO. All with a Pox—no Mrs. *Jezebel*, that's not all; there's Two Hundred Pound Due to my self for Tea, Coffee and Chocolet, which my Journey-man has Confess'd since your Roguery came out—that you have Imbezell'd, Huswife, you have; so, this comes of your keeping Quality Company—e'en let them keep you now, for I have done with you, you shall come no more within my Doors I promise you.

MRS. SAGO. Oh! Kill me rather; I never did it with Design to part with you, indeed Puddy. (*Sobbing.*)

MR. SAGO. No, no, I believe not whilst I was Worth a Groat. Oh!

Enter Sir James.

SIR JAMES COURTLY. How! Mrs. *Sago* in Tears, and my honest Friend in Ruffins Hands; the meaning of this.

MR. SAGO.† Oh! Sir *James*—my Hypocritical Wife is as much a Wife as any Wife in the City—I'm Arrested here in an Action of a Thousand Pound, that she has taken up Goods for, and Gam'd away; get out of my sight, get out of my sight, I say.

MRS. SAGO. Indeed and indeed. (*Sobbing.*) Dear Puddy but I cannot—no, here will I Hang for ever on this Neck. (*Flies about his Neck.*)

MR. SAGO.† Help, Murder, Murder, why, why, what will you Collar me?[1]

---

1   To fetter or constrain around the neck.

SIR JAMES COURTLY. Right Woman, I must try to make up this Breach—Oh! Mr. *Sago*, you are unkind—'tis pure Love that thus Transports your Wife, and not such Base Designs as you Complain of.

MR. SAGO.† Yes, yes, and she run me in Debt out of pure Love too no doubt.

MRS. SAGO. So it was Pudd.

MR. SAGO. What was it? (Ha, Mistress) out of love to me that you have undone me? Thou, thou, thou, I don't know what to call thee bad enough.

MRS. SAGO. You won't hear your Keckey out, Dear Pudd, it was out of Love for Play,—but for Lo, Lo, Love to you, Dear Pudd; if you'll forgive me I'll ne'er play again. (*Crying and Sobbing all the while.*)

SIR JAMES COURTLY. Nay, now Sir, you must forgive her.

MR. SAGO.† What, forgive her that would send me to Jayl?

SIR JAMES COURTLY. No, no, there's no Danger of that, I'll Bail you, Mr. *Sago*, and try to Compound those Debts.—You know me Officers.

BALIFFS. Very well, Sir *James*, your Worship's Word is sufficient.

SIR JAMES COURTLY. There's you Fees, then leave here your Prisoner, I'll see him forth coming.

BALIFFS. With all our Hearts; your Servant, Sir. (*Exit.*)

MR. SAGO. Ah thou wicked Woman, how I have doated on those Eyes! How often have I kneel'd to kiss that Hand! Ha, is not this true, Keckey?

MRS. SAGO. Yes, Deary, I, I, I, I do confess it.

MR. SAGO. Did ever I refuse to grant whatever thou ask'd me?

MRS. SAGO. No, never, Pudd—(*Weeps still.*)

MR. SAGO. Might'st thou not have eaten Gold, as the Saying is? Ha?—Oh Keecky, Keecky! (*Ready to weep.*)

SIR JAMES COURTLY. Leave Crying, and wheedle him, Madam, wheedle him.

MRS. SAGO. I do confess it, and cann't you forgive your Keckey then that you have been so Tender of, that you so often confest your Heart has jump'd up to your Mouth when you have heard my Beauty prais'd.

MR. SAGO. So it has I profess, Sir *James*—I begin to melt,—I do; I am a good-nature'd Fool, that's the Truth on't: But if I should forgive you, what would you do to make me Amends? For that Fair Face, if I turn you out of Doors, will quickly be a cheaper Drug than any in my Shop.

SIR JAMES COURTLY. And not maintain her half so well;— promise largely, Madam. (*To Mrs. Sago.*)

MRS. SAGO. I'll Love you for ever, Deary.

MR. SAGO. But you'll Jigg to *Covent-Garden* again.

MRS. SAGO. No, indeed I won't come within the Air on't, but take up with City Acquaintance, rail at the Court, and go Twice a Week with Mrs. *Outside* to *Pin-makers-hall.*

MR. SAGO. That would rejoice my Heart. (*Ready to weep.*)

SIR JAMES COURTLY. See, if the good Man is not ready to weep; your last Promise has conquer'd.—Come, come, Buss and be Friends and end the Matter.—I'm glad the Quarrel is made up, or I had had her upon my Hands. (*Aside.*)

MRS. SAGO. Pudd, don't you hear Sir *James*, Pudd?

MR. SAGO. I can't hold no longer,—yes, I do hear him,—come then to the Arms of thy n'own Pudd. (*Runs into one another's Arms.*)

SIR JAMES COURTLY. Now all's well; and for your Comfort Lady *Reveller* is by this Time married to my Lord *Worthy*, and there will be no more Gaming I assure you in that House.

MR. SAGO. Joy upon Joys. Now if these Debts were but Accommodated, I should be happier than ever; I should indeed Kickky.

SIR JAMES COURTLY. Leave that to me, Mr. *Sago*, I have won Part of your Wife's Money, and will that Way restore it to you.

MR. SAGO. I thank you, good Sir *James*, I believe you are the First Gamester that ever Refunded.

MRS. SAGO. Generously done,—Fortune has brought me off this Time, and I'll never trust her more.

SIR JAMES COURTLY. But see the Bride and Bridegroom.

Enter Lord Worthy *and Lady* Reveller, *Lady* Lucy, Buckle, Alpiew.

LADY LUCY. This Match which I have now been Witness to, is what I long have wish'd, your Course of Life must of Necessity be chang'd.

LADY REVELLER. Ha, Sir *James* here!—Oh if you love me, my Lord let us avoid that Brute, you must not meet him.

SIR JAMES COURTLY. Oh, there's no Danger, Madam.—My Lord, I wish you Joy with all my Heart; we only quarrell'd to make you Friends, Madam, ha, ha, ha.

LADY REVELLER. What, am I trick'd into a Marriage then?

LORD WORTHY. Not against your Will, I hope.

LADY REVELLER. No, I forgive you; tho' had I been aware of it, it should have cost you a little more Pains.

LORD WORTHY. I wish I could return thy Plot, and make this Lady thine, Sir *James*.

SIR JAMES COURTLY. Then I should be paid with Interest, my Lord.

LADY LUCY. My Fault is Consideration you know, I must think a little longer on't.

SIR JAMES COURTLY. And my whole Study shall be to improve those Thoughts to my own Advantage.

MR. SAGO. I wish your Ladiship Joy, and hope I shall keep my Kickey to my self now.

LADY REVELLER. With all my Heart Mr. *Sago*, she has had ill Luck of late, which I am sorry for.

MR. SAGO. My Lord *Worthy* will you confine your Ladiship from Play as well as I, and my Injunction will be more easie when I have your Example.

BUCKLE. Nay 'tis Time to throw up the Cards when the Games out.

Enter Sir Richard, *Captain* Hearty, Lovely *and* Valeria.

CAPTAIN HEARTY. Well, Sir *James*, the Danger's over, we have doubled the Cape,[1] and my Kinsman is Sailing directly to the Port.

SIR JAMES COURTLY. A Boon Voyage.

---

1 The Cape of Good Hope, South Africa, also known as the Cape of Storms, was a treacherous stretch of water mid-way on the voyages to India of the East India Company vessels.

SIR RICHARD PLAINMAN. 'Tis done, and my Heart is at Ease.—Did you ever see such a perverse Baggage, look in his Face I say, and thank your Stars, for their best influences gave you this Husband.

ENSIGN LOVELY. Will not *Valeria* look upon me? She us'd to be more Kind when we have fish'd for Eels† in Vinegar.

VALERIA. My *Lovely*, is it thee? And has natural Sympathy forborn to inform my Sense thus Long? (*Flies to him.*)

SIR RICHARD PLAINMAN. How! how! This *Lovely*? What does it prove the Ensign I have so carefully avoided!

ENSIGN LOVELY. Yes Sir, the same; I hope you may be brought to like a Land Soldier as well as a Seaman.

SIR RICHARD PLAINMAN. And, Captain, have you done this?

CAPTAIN HEARTY. Yes, Faith, she was too whimsical for our Element; her hard Words might have Conjur'd up a Storm for ought I know—so I have set her ashore.

LADY REVELLER. What, my Uncle deceiv'd with his Stock of Wisdom? Ha, ha, ha.

BUCKLE. Here's such a Coupling, Mrs. *Alpiew*, han't you a Month's Mind?[1]

ALPIEW. Not to you I assure you.

BUCKLE. I was but in Jest, Child, say nay when you're ask'd.

SIR JAMES COURTLY. The principal Part of this Plot was mine, Sir *Richard*.

SIR RICHARD PLAINMAN. Wou'd 'twas in my Power to hang you for't. (*Aside.*)

SIR JAMES COURTLY. And I have no Reason to doubt you should repent it, he is a Gentleman, tho' a younger Brother, he loves your Daughter, and she him, which has the best Face of Happiness in a married State; you like a Man of Honour, and he has as much as any one, that I assure you, Sir *Richard*.

SIR RICHARD PLAINMAN. Well, since what's past is past Recal I had as good be satisfied as not, therefore take her, and bless ye together.

LORD WORTHY. So now each Man's Wish is Crown'd, but mine with double Joy.

---

1 "An inclination, fancy" (*OED*).

CAPTAIN HEARTY. Well said, Sir *Richard*, let's have a Bowl of Punch, and Drink to the Bridegroom's good Voyage to Night,—steady, steady, ha, ha.

MR. SAGO. I'll take a Glass with you Captain,—I reckon my self a Bridegroom too.

BUCKLE. I doubt Kickey won't find him such. (*Aside.*)

MRS. SAGO. Well,—poor Keckky's bound to good Behaviour, or she had lost quite her Puddy's Favour.

> *Shall I for this repine at Fortune?—No.*
> *I'm glad at Heart that I'm forgiven so.*
> *Some Neighbours Wives have but too lately shown,*
> *When Spouse had left 'em all their Friends were flown.*
> *Then all you Wives that wou'd avoid my Fate.*
> *Remain contented with your present State.*

FINIS.

Textual Notes

See also *A Note on the Text*, above, p. 35.

Dedication
p. 41   ridiculing] D1; rediculing Q1
               Intemperance] D1; Intemperence Q1
               scandalous] D1; scandelous Q1

p. 42   ridicule] D1; Redicule, Q1

Prologue
p. 43   hunger] D1; hungar, Q1

p. 44   plenteous] D1; plentious Q1

Epilogue
p. 45   vent'ring] D1; ventring, Q1
               Yond] D1; Yon'd, Q1
               maul] D1; mauls, Q1

Dramatis Personae
p. 47   Inveterate] D1; Inverate, Q1
               Mrs. Sago] D1; Mrs. Sogo, Q1

The Basset Table
p. 50   Tour] D1; Tower, Q1

p. 51   explain] D1; explain'd, Q1
               Admire] Q1; pursue, D1
               bred] D1; bread, Q1

p. 52   Leva] Q2, Q3; Levn, Q1
               too] D1; to, Q1
               I resolve to quit your House] Q1; I resolve you shall quit
               my House, D1

| p. 55 | Crowd] D1; Croud, Q1 |
| | difference] D1; differerence, Q1 |

p. 56	Lovely] D1; Lovel, Q1
	And all her Experiments on Frogs, Fish—and Flies, ha,
	ha, ha, without the least Contradiction] attributed to Sir
	James Courtly, 1735; attributed Ensign Lovely Q1, D1

| p. 57 | chiefest] Q1; strongest, D1 |
| | lov'd Cant] 1735; lov'd, can't , Q1, D1 |

| p. 58 | Intrigue] D1; Intreague, Q1 |
| | lie] 1735; lyes, Q1; lies, D1 |

p. 60	Digressions] D1; Disgressions, Q1
	handsome] D1; handsom, Q1
	pursu'd] D1; persu'd, Q1

| p. 61 | imaginable] D1; immaginable, Q1 |

| p. 62 | (*Is going and comes back often.*) follows Lord Worthy's line] |
| | D1; follows Alpiew's 'I will', Q1 |

p. 65	Valeria] D1; Veleria, Q1
	Philosophy] D1; Peilosophy, Q1
	suits] D1; Sutes, Q1

| p. 66 | handsome] D1; handsom, Q1 |
| | Gaul] Q1, D1; Soul] 1735 |

p. 67	*Descartes*] D1, *Discartes* Q1
	Mistress] D1, Mrs., Q1
	converse] D1; converss, Q1
	you're] D1; you'r, Q1

| p. 69 | Pedant] D1; Pedaunt, Q1 |

| p. 70 | listen] D1; lissen, Q1 |

p. 73   guess'd] D1; guest'd, Q1

p. 74   there's] D1; ther's, Q1

p. 75   too] D1; to, Q1

p. 82   Intrigues] D1; Intreigues, Q1

p. 83   we] Q1; Women, D1

p. 84   Lady Reveller] 1735; Mr. Buckle] Q1, D1

p. 87   Combat] D1; Combate, Q1

p. 88   too] D1; to, Q1

p. 91   ACT IV] D1; ACT III, Q1

p. 93   SIR RICHARD PLAINMAN.] D1; SIR JAMES
         COURTLY., Q1
         Captain launch off a round Lie or Two.] Ensign Lovely
         D1; Captain launch off a round Lie or Two. (*Aside to the
         Ensign.*)], end of Sir Richard's speech, Q1

p. 95   Endeavour] D1; Eedeavour, Q1

p. 96   *Bait's gone*] D1; *Baits gon*, Q1

p. 98   Vicious] D1; Vitious, Q1
         Terms] Q1; Term, Q2

p. 100   unlucky] D1; unluckly, Q1

p. 100   Fac'd] D1; Fac't, Q1

p. 101   Fac't] Q1; Face't, D1

p. 108   Piece] Q1; iece, Q2

p. 109	thee] D1; the, Q1
p. 110	MR. SAGO] D1; MRS. SAGO, Q1
p. 111	MR. SAGO] D1; MRS. SAGO, Q1
	MR. SAGO] D1; MRS. SAGO, Q1
p. 112	MR. SAGO] 1760; MRS. SAGO, Q1, D1, 1735, 1736
p. 115	Eels] D1; Eals, Q1

Appendix A: Female Education

[Valeria, with her keen interest in natural philosophy, would have been recognized by contemporary audiences as that unusual creature, a learned lady. In the 1690s, the debate about the extent and purpose of women's education had been reignited, in part by Mary Astell's passionate polemic excerpted below. Elite and genteel women might receive an education at home, but there was a growing interest in schooling for girls from a broader range of society. Bathsua Makin had argued the case for educating young women of the middling sort, and her popular pamphlet on the benefits of female education, excerpted here, also doubled as an advertisement for her school in Twickenham.]

1. From Mary Astell, *A Serious Proposal to the Ladies ... In Two Parts* (1697): 36-38, 285-86

[Mary Astell (1666-1731), a philosopher and pamphleteer, was part of a high-church Anglican and Tory group. Amongst other works she wrote two serious polemics on the subjection of women, *A Serious Proposal to the Ladies ... In Two Parts* (1694; 1697) which is excerpted here, and *Some Reflections Upon Marriage* (1700). Her plan for the founding of a secular monastery for the education of women was relentlessly mocked because of its Catholic overtones and the implied celibacy of the female inhabitants.]

Now as to the Proposal, it is to erect a Monastery, or if you will (to avoid giving offence to the scrupulous and injudicious, by names which tho' innocent in themselves, have been abus'd by superstitious Practices,) we will call it a Religious Retirement, and such as shall have a double aspect, being not only a Retreat from the World for those who desire that advantage, but likewise, an Institution and previous discipline, to fit us to do the greatest good in it; such an Institution as this (if I do not mightily deceive my self) would be the most probable method to amend the present, and improve the future Age.... Such as are willing in a more peculiar and undisturb'd manner, to attend the great business they came into the world about, the service of GOD and improvement of their own Minds, may find a convenient and blissful recess from the noise and hurry of the world. A world so cumbersom, so infectious, that altho' thro' the grace of GOD and their own strict watchfulness, they are kept from sinking down into its corruptions, 'twill however damp their flight to heav'n, hinder them from attaining any eminent pitch of Vertue.

You are therefore Ladies, invited into a place, where you shall suffer no other confinement, but to be kept out of the road of sin: You shall not be depriv'd of your Grandeur but only exchange the vain Pomps and Pageantry of the world, empty Titles and Forms of State, for the true and solid Greatness of being able to despise them. You will only quit the Chat of insignificant people for an ingenious Conversation; the froth of flashy Wit for real Wisdom; idle tales for instructive discourses.

...

...since such Seminaries[1] are thought proper for the Men, since they enjoy the fruits of those Noble Ladies Bounty who were the foundresses of several of their Colleges, why shou'd we not think that such ways of Education wou'd be as advantageous to the Ladies? or why shou'd we despair of finding some among them who will be as kind to their own Sex as their Ancestors have been to the other? Some Objections against this design have already been consider'd, and those which I have since met with are either too trifling to deserve a serious Answer, or too illnatur'd not to require a severer than I care to give them. They must either be very Ignorant or very Malicious who pretend that we wou'd imitate Foreign Monastries, or object against us the Inconveniencies that they are subject to; a little attention to what they read might have convinc'd them that our Institution is rather *Academical* than *Monastic*. So that it is altogether beside the purpose, to say 'tis too Recluse, or preju-

---

1 A seminary could mean a school or place of education, but in the sixteenth and seventeenth centuries it also suggested a college for training Catholic priests, often Jesuits, for missionary activity. Astell takes care to defuse this idea in this passage.

dicial to an Active Life; 'tis as far from that as a Ladys Practising at home is from being a hindrance to her dancing at Court. For an Active Life consists not barely in *Being in the World*, but in *doing much Good in it*: And therefore it is fit we Retire a little, to furnish our Understandings with useful Principles, to set our Inclinations right, and to manage our Passions, and when this is well done, but not till then, we may safely venture out.

2. Satire on Mary Astell, Jonathan Swift and Richard Steele, *The Tatler*, 32, June 21-23, 1709

[Astell's proposal for a female educational retreat remained a powerful image in the English imagination, particularly because of its similarities to French, Catholic counterparts. As late as 1709, Jonathan Swift (1667-1745) and Richard Steele (ca.1672-1729), at this stage both Whig writers and satirists, mocked her model for its religious overtones. *The Tatler*, a thrice-weekly periodical started by Steele in April 1709, offered social and literary commentary that elsewhere included praise for the behaviour of educated and informed women.]

There were some years since a set of these [Platonic] ladies who were of quality, and gave out, that virginity was to be their state of life during this mortal condition, and therefore resolved to join their fortunes, and erect a nunnery. The place of residence was pitched upon; and a pretty situation, full of natural falls and risings of waters, with shady coverts, and flowery arbours, was approved by seven of the founders. There were as many of our sex who took the liberty to visit those mansions of intended severity; among others, a famous rake of that time, who had the grave way to an excellence. He came in first; but upon seeing a servant coming towards him, with a design to tell him, this was no place for him or his companions, up goes my grave impudence to the main: "Young woman," said he, "if any of the ladies are in the way on this side of the house, pray carry us on the other side towards the gardens: we are, you must know, gentlemen that are travelling in England; after which we shall go into foreign parts, where some of us have already been." Here, he bows in the most humble manner, and kissed the girl, who knew not how to behave to such a sort of carriage. He goes on: "Now you must know we have an ambition to have it to say, that we have a Protestant nunnery in England:" ... His friend advances, and so on, till that they had all saluted her. By this means, the poor girl was in the middle of the crowd of these fellows, at a loss what to do, without courage to pass through them; and the Platonicks, at several peep-holes, pale, trembling, and fretting. Rake perceived they were observed, and therefore took care to keep Suky in chat with questions concerning their way of life; when appeared at last Madonella,[1] a lady who had writ a fine book concerning the recluse life, and was the projectrix of the foundation. She approaches into the hall; and Rake, know-ing the dignity of his own mien and aspect, goes deputy from his company. She begins, "Sir, I am obliged to follow the servant, who was sent out to know, what affair could make strangers press upon a solitude which we, who are to inhabit this place, have devoted to Heaven and our own thoughts?" "Madam," replies Rake, with an air of great distance, mixed with a certain indifference, by which he could dissemble dissimulation, "your great intention has made more noise in the world than you design it should; and we travellers, who have seen many foreign institutions of this kind, have a curiosity to see, in its first rudiments, this seat of primitive piety; for such it must be called by future ages, to the eternal honour of the found-ers. I have read Madonella's excellent and seraphic discourse on this subject." The lady immediately answers, "If what I have said could have contributed to raise any thoughts in you that may make for the advancement of intellectual and divine conversation, I should think myself extremely happy." He immediately fell back with the profoundest veneration; then advancing, "Are you then that admired lady? If I may approach lips which have uttered things so sacred—" He salutes her. His friends follow his example. The devoted within stood in amazement where this would end, to see Madonella receive their address and company.... [W]ithout entering into further par-ticulars, there was hardly one of them but was a mother or father that day twelve-month.

---

1 Madonella: a mock reference to Mary Astell, who complains about the *Tatler*'s por-trayal of her in a later pamphlet, *Bart'lemy Fair* (London, 1709).

3. From Daniel Defoe, *An Essay upon Projects* (1697): 282-83, 284-87, 292-93, 302-03

[Daniel Defoe (1660-1731), a writer and satirist, is perhaps best remembered today for his satirical novel, *Robinson Crusoe* (1719). In *An Essay upon Projects*, one of his first works, he offered pragmatic and satirical views of banks, projectors, and lotteries, as well as female education and academies in general.]

Under this Head of Academies I might bring a Project for *An Academy for Women.*

I have often thought of it as one of the most barbarous Customs in the world, considering us as a Civiliz'd and a Christian Countrey, that we deny the advantages of Learning to Women. We reproach the Sex every day with Folly and Impertinence, while I am confident, had they the advantages of Education equal to us, they wou'd be guilty of less than our selves.

One wou'd wonder indeed how it shou'd happen that Women are conversible at all, since they are only beholding to Natural Parts for all their Knowledge. Their Youth is spent to teach them to Stitch and Sew, or make Bawbles: They are taught to Read indeed, and perhaps to Write their Names, or so; and that is the heighth of a Woman's Education. And I wou'd but ask any who slight the Sex for their Understanding, What is a Man (a Gentleman I mean) good for, that is taught no more?

...

The Capacities of Women are suppos'd to be greater, and their Senses quicker than those of the Men; and what they might be capable of being bred to, is plain from some Instances of Female Wit, which this Age is not without; which upbraids us with Injustice and looks as if we deni'd Women the advantages of Education, for Fear they shou'd vye with the Men in their Improvements.

To remove this Objection, and that Women might have at least a needful Opportunity of Education in all sorts of Useful Learning, I propose the Draught of an Academy for that purpose.

I know 'tis dangerous to make Publick Appearances of the Sex; they are not either to be *confin'd* or *expos'd*; the first will disagree with their Inclinations, and the last with their Reputations; and therefore it is somewhat difficult; and I doubt a Method propos'd by an Ingenious Lady, in a little Book, call'd, *Advice to the Ladies*,[1] would be found impracticable. For, saving my Respect to the Sex, the Levity, which perhaps is a little peculiar to them, at least in their Youth, will not bear the Restraint; and I am satisfi'd, nothing but the heighth of Bigotry can keep up a Nunnery: Women are extravagantly desirous of going to Heaven, and will punish their *Pretty Bodies* to get thither; but nothing else will do it; and even in that case sometimes it falls out that *Nature will prevail*.

When I talk therefore of an Academy for Women, I mean both the Model, the Teaching, and the Government, different from what is propos'd by that Ingenious Lady, for whose Proposal I have a very great Esteem, and also a great Opinion of her Wit; different too from all sorts of Religious Confinement, and above all, from *Vows of Celibacy*.

Wherefore the Academy I propose should differ but little from Publick Schools, wherein such Ladies as were willing to study, shou'd have all the advantages of Learning suitable to their Genius.

...

The Persons who Enter, shou'd be taught all sorts of Breeding suitable to both their Genius and their Quality; and in particular, *Musick* and *Dancing*, which it wou'd be cruelty to bar the Sex of, because they are their Darlings: But besides this, they shou'd be taught Languages, as particularly *French* and *Italian*; and I wou'd venture the Injury of giving a Woman more Tongues than one.

They shou'd, as a particular Study, be taught all the Graces of Speech, and all the necessary Air of Conversation; which our common Education is so defective in, that I need not expose it: They shou'd be brought to read Books, and especially History, and so to read as to make them understand the World, and be able to know and judge of things when they hear of them.

---

1 Mary Astell's proposal in *A Serious Proposal*; see above, A1.

To such whose Genius wou'd lead them to it, I wou'd deny no sort of Learning; but the chief thing in general is to cultivate the Understandings of the Sex, that they may be capable of all sorts of Conversation; that their Parts and Judgments being improv'd, they may be as Profitable in their Conversation as they are Pleasant.

Women, in my observation, have little or no difference in them, but as they are, or are not distinguish'd by Education. Tempers indeed may in some degree influence them, but the main distinguishing part is their Breeding.

...

And herein it is that I take upon me to make such a bold Assertion, That all the World are mistaken in their Practice about Women: For I cannot think that God Almighty ever made them so delicate, so glorious Creatures, and furnish'd them with such Charms, so Agreeable and so Delightful to Mankind, with Souls capable of the same Accomplishments with Men, and all to be only Stewards of our Houses, *Cooks and Slaves.*

Not that I am for exalting the Female Government in the least: But, in short, *I wou'd have Men take Women for Companions, and Educate them to be fit for it.* A Woman of Sense and Breeding will scorn as much to encroach upon the Prerogative of the Man, as a Man of Sense will scorn to oppress the *Weakness* of the Woman. But if the Womens Souls were refin'd and improv'd by Teaching, that word wou'd be lost; to say, *The Weakness of the Sex,* as to Judgment, wou'd be Nonsense; for Ignorance and Folly wou'd be no more to be found among Women than Men.

4. From Bathsua Makin, *An Essay to Revive the Ancient Education of Gentlewomen in Religion, Manners, Arts and Tongues* (1673): 3-4, 22, 24-25

[Bathsua Makin (1600-75) had been tutor to Princess Elizabeth, Charles I's daughter, amongst other aristocratic ladies. Towards the end of her life she wrote this lively treatise, celebrating learned women in history and critiquing the teaching methods of Lily's

Grammar. The volume ends with a postscript which alerts the reader that just such an education as Makin recommends for girls is available at her school in Twickenham, for the annual sum of £20.]

To all Ingenious and Vertuous Ladies, more especially to her Highness the Lady Mary, Eldest Daughter to his Royal Highness the Duke of York.

Custom, when it is inveterate, hath a mighty influence: it hath the force of Nature it self. The Barbarous custom to breed Women low, is grown general amongst us, and hath prevailed so far, that it is verily believed (especially amongst a sort of debauched Sots) that Women are not endued with such Reason, as Men; nor capable of improvement by Education, as they are. It is lookt upon as a monstrous thing, to pretend the contrary. A Learned Woman is thought to be a Comet, that bodes Mischief, when ever it appears. To offer to the World the liberal Education of Women is to deface the Image of God in Man, it will make Women so high, and men so low, like Fire in the House-top, it will set the whole world in a Flame.

These things and worse then these, are commonly talked of, and verily believed by many, who think themselves wise Men: to contradict these is a bold attempt; where the Attempter must expect to meet with much opposition. Therefore, Ladyes, I beg the candid Opinion of your Sex, whose Interest I assert.... Women were formerly Educated in the knowledge of Arts and Tongues, and by their Education, many did rise to a great height in Learning. Were Women thus Educated now, I am confident the advantage would be very great: The Women would have Honour and Pleasure, their Relations Profit, and the whole Nation Advantage. I am very sensible it is an ill time to set on foot this Design: wherein not only Learning but Vertue it self is scorn'd and neglected, as pedantick things, fit only for the Vulgar. I know no better way to reform these Exorbitancies, than to perswade Women to scorn those Toyes and Trifles, they now spend their time about, and to attempt higher things, here offered: This will either reclaim the Men; or make them ashamed to claim the Sovereignty over such as are more Wise and Vertuous than themselves.

Were a competent number of Schools erected to Educate Ladyes ingenuously, methinks I see how asham'd Men would be of their

Ignorance, and how industrious the next Generation would be to wipe off their Reproach.

I expect to meet with many Scoffes and Taunts from inconsiderate and illiterate Men, that prize their own Lusts and Pleasure more than your Profit and Content. I shall be the less concern'd at these, so long as I am in your favour; and this discourse may be a Weapon in your hands to defend yourselves, whilst you endeavour to polish your Souls, that you may glorify God, and answer the end of your Creation, to be meet helps to your Husbands. Let not your Ladiships be offended, that I do not (as some have wittily done) plead for Female Preeminence. To ask too much is the way to be denied all. God hath made Man the Head, if you be educated and instructed, as I propose, I am sure you will acknowledge it, and be satisfied that you are helps, that your Husbands do consult and advise with you (which if you be wise they will be glad of) and that your Husbands have the casting-Voice, in whose determinations you will acquiesce.

...Care ought to be taken by us to Educate Women in Learning.

That I may be more distinct in what I intend, I shall distinguish of Women,

Women are of two sorts, {RICH} Of good natural Parts.
                          {POOR} Of low Parts.

I do not mean, that it is necessary to the *esse*, to the *subsistence*, or to the Salvation of Women, to be thus educated. Those that are mean in the World, have not an opportunity for this Education: Those that are of low Parts, though they may have opportunity, cannot reach this; *Ex quovis ligno non fit Minerva*: My meaning is, Persons that God hath blessed with the things of this World, that have competent natural Parts, ought to be educated in Knowledge; That is, it is much better they should spend the time of their Youth, to be competently instructed in those things usually taught to Gentlewomen in Schools, and the overplus of their time to be spent in gaining Arts, and Tongues, and useful Knowledge, rather than to trifle away so many precious minutes meerly to polish Hands and Feet, to curl their Locks, to dress and trim their Bodies; and in the mean time to neglect their Souls, and not at all, or very little to endeavour to know God, Jesus Christ, Themselves, and the things of Nature, Arts and Tongues, subservient to these. I do not deny but Women ought to be brought up to a comely and decent carriage, to their Needle, to Neatness, to understand all those things that do particularly belong to their Sex. But when these things are competently cared for, and where there are Endowments of Nature and leasure, then higher things ought to be endeavoured after.

...

If any desire distinctly to know what they should be instructed in?

I Answer, I cannot tell where to begin to admit Women, nor from what part of Learning to exclude them, in regard of their Capacities. The whole *Encyclopedeia* of Learning may be useful some way or other to them. Respect indeed is to be had to the Nature and Dignity of each Art and Science, as they are more or less subservient to Religion, and may be useful to them in their station. I would not deny them the knowledge of Grammar and Rhetorick, because they dispose to speak handsomly. Logick must be allowed, because it is the Key to all Sciences. Physick, especially Visibles, as Herbs, Plants, Shrubs, Drugs &c. must be studyed, because this will exceedingly please themselves, and fit them to be helpful to others. The Tongues ought to be studyed, especially the *Greek* and *Hebrew*, these will enable to the better understanding of the Scriptures.

The Mathematicks, more especially Geography, will be useful; this puts life into History. Musick, Painting, Poetry &c. are a great ornament and pleasure. Some things that are more practical, are not so material, because publick Employments in the Field and Courts, are usually denyed to Women: Yet some have not been inferior to many men even in these things also. Witness *Semiramis* amongst the *Babylonians*; The Queen of *Sheba* in *Arabia*; *Miriam* and *Debora* among the *Israelites*; *Katherine de Medices* in *France*; Queen *Elizabeth* in *England*....

In these late Times there are several instances of Women, when their Husbands were serving their King and Countrey, defended their Houses, and did all things, as Souldiers, with Prudence and Valour, like Men.

They appeared before Committees, and pleaded their own Causes with good success.

This kind of Education will be very useful to Women.

5. From Mary Chudleigh, *Essay on Several Subjects in Prose and Verse* (London, 1710): 1-2, 10-11, 17-18

[Mary Lee, Lady Chudleigh (1656-1710), a devout Anglican, probably knew Mary Astell and published three defences of women during her lifetime. In this essay she summons, in poetry and prose, the example of learned ladies from history, and illustrates the benefits of a broad education for her contemporaries.]

Of *KNOWLEDGE.*
To the Ladies.

When I look abroad into the World, and take a Survey of the Rational Nature, it grieves me to see what a vast Disproportion there is as to intellectual Endowments between the Men and Us: 'Tis a mortifying Prospect to see them exalted to such a tow'ring Height, rais'd so infinitely above the generality of our Sex. Some few indeed may vie with them, may shine bright in the Firmament of *Knowledge*: But what are they to the surrounding Splendors, to the Multitude of Lights? they are lost in the glorious Crowd, and cannot be retriev'd without a narrow Inspection, an attentive View! I wish I could perswade all, at least the greatest part of my Sex, those whose Circumstances do not necessarily oblige them to lower Cares, to put in for a Share, to enter their Claims, and not permit the Men any longer to monopolize the Perfections of the Mind, to ingross the Goods of the Understanding: I would not have them suffer themselves to be willingly dispossess'd of their Reason, and shut out of the Commonwealth of Learning: Neither would I have them so far impos'd on, as to be made to believe, that they are incapable of great Attainments. We have already given noble and undeniable Instances of the contrary, and can produce a long Catalogue of illustrious Names, can boast of *Ladies*, who have been as famous for their *Knowledge* as their *Vertue*.

...

In order to the raising our Thoughts to such sublime Speculations, 'tis necessary that we should be able to form to our selves clear Ideas, should have right conceptions of those Things on which we contemplate, to the Attainment of which Logick will be requisite; 'twill teach us to think regularly, to reason justly, to distinguish between Truth and Falshood, Things that are Simple, and such as are Compounded; Things that are Contingent, from such as are Necessary. And something of Geometry will be useful to qualifie and prepare our Minds for the Contemplation of Truth, and for the profitable Reading of any Books: 'Twill enable us to fix our Thoughts, and give a check to that quickness of Imagination which is seldom consistent with solidity of Judgment. Physicks ought to be our next Study, that will show us Nature, as she variously displays her self, as she manifests her self in material Objects, explains to us her surprizing *Phænomena*, instruct us heedfully to consider all her wonderful Productions, and trace infinite Wisdom and Power thro' the immense Space, from the Heights Above, to the Depths Below; from the glorious Orbs which roll over our Heads, to the minutest Insect that crawls under our Feet; discover to us Beauties which Art can never imitate, and which common Spectators do not observe. From the Consideration of those Divine Attributes which conspicuously shine in the visible Creation, we may ascend to the Metaphysicks, which is the Noblest, the most elevated Part of Science, that on which all the rest depend; it raises us above sensible Objects, advances us to Things purely Intellectual, and treats of Being, as abstracted from Matter: 'Twill perfect our Knowledge, and brighten our Reason; enable us to proceed in our researches after Truth, on steady and unerring Principles, and give us clearer and more distinct views of the adorable Excellencies of the Divine Nature. Geography will make us acquainted with the Earth we inhabit, will mark out its several Regions, and show us how one Part is divided from another either by Seas, Rivers, or Mountains;

'twill also be of use to abate our Pride, by representing to us how little and inconsiderable a Part our Globe is of the mighty Whole, and yet as despicably small as 'tis, it appears unmeasurably Great, if compar'd with that Point, that nothing on which we live.

...

Decency requires that we should take some Care of our Dress, and the Necessities of Nature oblige us to eat and drink; but then we must do it without a studied Luxury, without an unbecoming Application of Mind, without being Slaves to our Palates, and valuing our selves on the number and variety of our Dishes: Neither do I think it a Fault to go sometimes to the Play-house, or divert our selves at Cards, provided they do not engross too much of our Time, which is one of the chief Reasons of my cautioning you against the last; not that I think there are others of almost an equal Weight, as their augmenting and avaritious Humour, and exciting our Passions, which we find by Experience they do in Persons that are not govern'd by their Reason: ... I would have my Sex as Wise, as Knowing, and as Virtuous, as they are by Nature capable of being; and if I can by my Advice, be so fortunate, as in the least to contribute to it, I shall think my self happy.

Appendix B: Gambling

1. From Charles Cotton, "Basset," *The Compleat Gamester* (London, 1710; fifth edition): 177-83

[Charles Cotton (1630-87) was a poet, translator, and pamphleteer. *The Compleat Gamester* was a very popular compendium of games with full instructions and went into multiple editions through the eighteenth century. The fifth edition, printed in 1710, was the first to include basset, indicating the game's rising popularity among the lower ranks of society.]

This Game, amongst all those on the Cards, is accounted to be the most Courtly, being properly, by the understanders of it, thought only fit for Kings and Queens, great Princes, Noble-men &c. to Play at by reason of such great Losses, or Advantages as may possibly be on one side or other, during the time of Play.

It is in its Nature not much unlike our late *Royal-Oak-Lottery*;[1] and as that, by the Lottery-man's having five Figures in two and thirty for himself, must certainly be a considerable Profit to him in length of Time, so here the Dealer that keeps the Bank having the first and last Card has his own dispose, and other considerable Priviledges in the Dealing the Cards, has (without doubt) a greater Prospect of Gaining, than those at Play: this was a Truth so acknowledged in *France*, that the King made a Public Edict, that the Priviledge of a *Talliere*, or one that keep the Bank at *Basset*, should only be allow'd to Principal Cadets, or Sons of great Families, supposing that whoever was so befriended as to be admitted to keep the Bank, must naturally in a very short time become possessor of a considerable Estate.

But all others for fear of ruining private Persons, and Families, are confin'd Politicly to a Twelve-peny Bank, tho' here they have the liberty of staking what they please.

---

1   The Royal Oak Lottery, established for the benefit of the fishing industry, was one of the few lotteries to escape regular abolition.

The Terms of the Game are these.

Talliere	*The Pay,*
Croupiere	*Alpiew*
Punter	*Sept-et-le-va*
The Fasse	*Quinze-et-le-va*
The Couch	*Trent-et-le-va,*
The Paroli	*Soissant-et-le-va,* &c.
The Masse	

The Explanation of the Terms.

1. The *Talliere* is he that keeps the Bank, who lays down a Sum of Mony before all those that Play, to answer every Winning Card that shall appear in his course of Dealing.

2. The *Croupiere* is one that is assistant to the *Talliere*, and stands by to supervise the losing Cards; that when there are a considerable Company at Play, he may not lose by over seeing any thing that might turn to his Profit.

3. The *Punter* is a Term for every one of the Gamesters that Play.

4. The *Fasse*, is the first Card that is turn'd up by the *Talliere*, belonging to the whole Pack, by which he gains the Vallue of the Mony that is laid down upon every Card of that sort by the Punters.

5. The *Couch* is a Term for the first Mony that every Punter puts upon each Card, every one that Plays having a Book of Thirteen several Cards before him, upon which he may lay his Mony more or less according to his Fancy.

6. The *Paroli* is a Term explain'd thus, that having won the *Couch* or first Stake, and having a mind to go on to get a *Sept-et-le-va*, you crook the Corner of your Card, letting your Mony lie without being paid the value of it by the *Talliere*.

7. The *Masse* is when you have won the *Couch*, or first Stake, and will venture more Mony upon the same Card ...

8. The *Pay* is when the *Punter* has won the *Couch* or first Stake ... and being fearful to make the *Paroli*, leaves off, for by going the *Pay* if the Card turns up wrong he loses nothing ...

9. The *Alpiew* is much the same thing as the *Paroli*, and like that Term us'd when a *Couch* is won by turning up, or crooking the corner of the winning Card.

10. *Sept-et-le-va* is the first great Chance that shews the advantages

of this Game, as for example: If the *Punter* has won the *Couch*, and then makes a *Paroli*, by crooking the corner of his Card, as is said before, and going on to a second Chance his winning Card turns up again, it comes to *Sept-et-le-va*, which is seven times as much as he laid down upon his Card.

11. *Quinze-et-le-va* as next in its turn is attending the *Punter's* Humour, who perhaps is resolv'd to follow his Fancy and still lay his Mony upon the same Card, which is done by crooking the third Corner of his Card, which coming up by the Dealing of the *Talliere*, makes him win fifteen times as much Mony as he Stak'd.

12. *Trent-et-le-va* succeeds *Quinze-et-le-va*, and is markt by the lucky *Punter*, by crooking or bending the end of the fourth corner of his winning Card, which coming up, makes him Purchaser of three and thirty times as much Mony as he laid down.

13. *Soissant-et-le-va* is the highest and greatest chance that can happen in the Game, for it pays Sixty seven times as much Mony as is Stak'd and is seldom won but by some lucky *Punter* who resolves to push the extream of his good Fortune to the height: It cannot be won but by the *Talliere's* dealing the Cards over again, which if his winning Card turns up, pays him with such a prodigious Advantage....

The order of the Game is thus.

They sit down round a Table, as many as please, the *Talliere* in the midst of them with the Bank of Mony before him, and the *Punters* each having a Book of thirteen Cards, laying down one or two, three or more as they please with Mony upon them, as Stakes, then he [*Talliere*] takes the Pack altogether in his hand and turns them up, the bottom Card appearing is called the *Fasse*, and pays him half the value of Mony laid down by the Punters upon any Card of that sort as has been said before.

The manner of the Play is thus.

After the *Fasse* is turn'd up and the *Talliere* and *Croupiere* have look'd round the Cards on the Table and taken half the Advantage of the Mony laid on them he [*Talliere*] proceeds with his Deal, and the next Card appearing, whither King, Queen, Ace, or whatever it may be, wins for the *Punter*, who may receive if he has laid Mony on such a sort of Card the value, or making *Paroli* go on to a *Sept-et-le-va*, as has been said, the Card after that wins for the *Talliere*, who takes Mony from each *Punter's* Card of that sort and brings it to his Bank.... so every other Card alternately winning and loosing till all the Pack be Dealt out but the last Card.

The last Card turn'd up (as I hinted before) is an Advantage to the *Talliere*, because by the Rule of the Game which was contriv'd for his Benefit tho' it be turn'd up and the *Punter* may happen to have stak'd upon one of the same sort, yet it is allow'd as one of his Dues in relation to his Office, and he pays nothing.

2. From Joseph Addison, *The Guardian*, 120, 29 July 1713

[Joseph Addison (1672–1719) was a Whig politician, writer, and dramatist, who collaborated with Richard Steele on *The Tatler, The Spectator,* and *The Guardian*. Addison contributed fifty-two papers, reflecting on social mores and party political matters, to *The Guardian*.]

COULD we look into the *Mind* of a Female Gamester, we should see it full of nothing but *Trumps* and *Mattadores*.[1] Her Slumbers are haunted with Kings, Queens and Knaves. The Day lies heavy upon her till the Play-Season returns, when for half a dozen Hours together all her Faculties are employed in Shuffling, Cutting, Dealing and Sorting out a Pack of Cards, and no Ideas to be discovered in a Soul which calls it self rational, excepting little square Figures of painted and spotted Paper. Was the Understanding, that Divine Part in our Composition, given for such an Use? Is it thus that we improve the greatest Talent Human Nature is endowed with? What would a Superior Being think, were he shown this intellectual Faculty in a Female Gamester, and at the same time told that it was by this she was distinguished from Brutes, and allied to Angels?

WHEN our Women thus fill their Imaginations with Pipps and Counters, I cannot wonder at the Story I have lately heard of a new-born Child that was *marked* with the five of Clubs.

---

1   Matadores: the highest trump cards.

THEIR *Passions* suffer no less by this Practice than their Understandings and Imaginations. What Hope and Fear, Joy and Anger, Sorrow and Discontent break out all at once in a fair Assembly upon so noble an Occasion as that of turning up a Card? Who can consider without a Secret Indignation that all those Affections of the Mind which should be consecrated to their Children, Husbands and Parents, are thus vilely prostituted and thrown away upon a Hand at Loo.[1]

...

I come in the next Place to consider the ill Consequences which Gaming has on the *Bodies* of our Female Adventurers. It is so ordered that almost every thing which corrupts the Soul decays the Body. The Beauties of the Face and Mind are generally destroyed by the same Means. This Consideration should have a particular Weight with the Female World, who were designed to please the Eye and attract the Regards of the other half of the Species. Now there is nothing that wears out a fine Face like the Vigils of the Card-Table, and those cutting Passions which naturally attend them. Hollow Eyes, haggard Looks, and pale Complexions, are the natural Inclinations of a Female Gamester. Her Morning Sleeps are not able to repair her Midnight Watchings. I have known a Woman carried off half dead from Bassette, and have many a time grieved to see a Person of Quality gliding by me in her Chair at two a Clock in the Morning, and looking like a Spectre amidst a glare of Flambeaux. In short, I never knew a thorough-paced Female Gamester hold her Beauty two Winters together.

BUT there is still another Case in which the Body is more endangered than in the former. All Play-Debts must be paid in Specie, or by an Equivalent. The Man that plays beyond his Income pawns his Estate; the Woman just finds out something else to Mortgage when her Pin-mony is gone: The Husband has his Lands to dispose of, the Wife her Person. Now when the Female Body is once *Dipp'd*, if the Creditor be very importunate, I leave my Reader to consider the Consequences.

---

1   Loo, or lanterloo, was a card game where a player who fails to take a trick or who breaks a rule pays a fine to the "loo," or pool.

3. From Jeremy Collier, *An Essay upon Gaming* (London, 1713): 22, 30-31, 35-36

[Jeremy Collier (1650-1726) was a non-juror Anglican clergy-man, pamphleteer, and social reformer, who also authored the anti-theatrical tract, *A Short View of the Immorality and Profaneness of the English Stage* (1698), excerpted in Appendix C. In the lively dialogue excerpted below, the social ills of gambling are vigorously displayed.]

Callimachus:[1] As to the Hazards, they are frightful, and suf-ficient to overset the Temper of better principled People than Gamesters commonly are. Have we not heard of Ladies losing hundreds of Guinea's at a Sitting? And others more slenderly stock'd, disfurnish their Husbands Studies, and play off the Books, which it may be help'd to feed them: And when the Women are thus Courageous, the Men conclude their own Sex calls for a bolder Liberty: That they ought to go farther in Danger, and appear more brave in the Methods of Ruin: Thus a *Manor* has been lost in an Afternoon, the *Suit* and *Service* follows the *Cast*, and the Right is transfer'd sooner than the Lawyer can draw the Conveyance.

...

Dolomedes: This Misfortune is nothing but shifting of Property, and putting the Prize into a new Hand: And is not this both a common and reasonable Remove? Why should Wealth be always lodg'd in the same Family? Why should not the Generality of Mankind come in for their Turn of Plenty and Figure? Why should not all the Sons of *Noah* have a Share in their Ancestors Patrimony? To reply, that the common Right has been lost long since by Division, and that Property is now confin'd to Birth and legal Settlement: To say this, is in effect to confess the Partiality of the *Constitution*, and to tell me a few

---

1   The pamphlet is a dialogue between the wise Callimachus, named after the Greek poet, and the careless sharper, Dolomedes, named after a spider.

People are born to make Beggars of the rest. This Inclosure is more than I can well digest: Pardon me, if I have not so much Deference for *Genealogy* and Elder Brothers, as this comes to.

Callimachus: I perceive you are not uninstructed in the *Levelling* Doctrine:[1] *Jack Straw* and *Watt Tyler*[2] would have argued at this rate.

...

Callimachus: Alas! the Man's Inclinations lye *Abroad*, and his Heart is stollen from his Business: His Thoughts are pre-engag'd and hurry'd, the Cards and Dice are playing in his Head, and he is ruminating on the Turns of Fortune at his last Adventure. It may be he came Home tir'd in the Morning, lyes recruiting in his Bed, and can't be spoken with at the Hours of Business: Thus this desperate Diversion is particularly fatal to a *Tradesman*; the Stock is sunk, the Credit blasted, and the Customers retire; the Man has no Brains left for Buying and Selling, nor any Time, unless for *Licence* and Losing his Money.

Dolomedes: What are we to have next?

Callimachus: From what has been discoursed, 'tis easy to infer that *Gaming* brings People into ill Company. 'Tis an Inlet to Drinking and Debauchery. Without any Reflexion upon *Dolomedes*, your *Gamesters* are commonly finish'd *Rakes*, and their *Morals* are as bad as their *Mystery*: For not to mention that they are early initiated, and well disciplin'd in running Riot: Not to mention this, 'tis Part of their Business to be exemplary this way, to spread the Infection, and teach what they practice.

---

1 The Levellers were a radical group of dissenters during the English Civil War, who argued for a secular democracy with the widest possible male franchise, religious toleration, and the abolition of the House of Lords. Their ideas influenced natural right theorists such as John Locke.

2 Jack Straw and Wat Tyler were leaders of the anti-tax Peasants' Revolt of 1381.

4. From Theophilus Lucas, *Memoirs of the Lives, Intrigues, and Comical Adventures of the most Famous Gamesters* (London, 1714): 66-67, 249-50

[Nothing is known of Theophilus Lucas, probably a pseudonym. *The Memoirs* are a collection of stories of rascals, royal consorts, and other celebrated characters, not all of whom were known for gaming. Whilst mostly fictitious, the stories reveal the other side to the moral debate about gambling; a delight in the cunning of the trickster figure.]

Colonel Panton ... was (as we have said before) a very great Gamester at Cards, by which Means he won a great deal of Money from the Duke of *Monmouth*, Duke of *Lauderdale*, and the late Duke of *Buckingham*; but one Day he was cunningly drawn in by Mrs. *Davis* (a mistress to King Charles II.)[1] who being visited by this Gamester, and entering into Play with him at *Basset*, she pull'd 150 Guineas out of a great Bag of Gold, saying, that as she found Fortune favour'd her in the first Game, she would venture next what she had lying by her. The Bulk of what was in the Bag, seeming to be not less than 14 or 1500 Guineas, the Colonel purposely lost the first Game, in hopes of winning all that Money before he left her; but she taking up the Stakes she had won, would not Play any more then, because, she said she never took any Diversion in Playing above one Set at a Time. *Panton* was much vex'd to see how he was taken in by a Woman for 150 Guineas, but how to help himself he could not tell; he took his Leave of her with an Air of Complacency, and went to seek out for a better Adventure. Not long after he paid another Visit to Mrs. *Davis*, with whom being engag'd at a Game of *Basset* again, he plac'd her Back towards a Looking-glass, so that as she held her Cards up, he could see what she had, and by this Stratagem (still used by old Sharpers upon young Gamesters) he won above 1100*l*. in Gold and Silver, and then laugh'd at her for her Folly.[2]

---

1   Mary Davis was a well-known performer on the early Restoration stage.

2   It is unlikely that the game referred to is basset, since players do not conceal their hand, but play and wager openly.

...

The Dutchess of Mazarin,[1] A Gamester ... she came over to England; where being mightily in favour with King *Charles* II, she lived to the height of Voluptuousness in all degrees; and for Gaming, her lodgings were more frequented than the *Groom*-Porters, in which she was as great a Proficient as any at that time; witness her winning at *Basset* of *Nell Gwin*[2] 1400 guineas in one night, and of the Dutchess of Portsmouth[3] of 8000*l.* in doing of which she exerted her utmost Cunning, and had the greatest Satisfaction, because they were her Rivals in the Royal Favour. The Monarch himself contributed also to her Advantage, being often taken in by her when he play'd. She would play as fair as any Person, when she found her Gamester play only upon the square, for she play'd so well that scarce any one could match her; but when she had a Sharp Gamester to deal with, she would play altogether upon the sharp at any Game upon the cards; and generally came off a Winner.

---

1 Hortense Mancini, Duchess of Mazarin (1646-99), niece of Louis XIV's chief minister, Cardinal Mazarin, travelled to England in 1675 and became a mistress of Charles II.

2 Nell Gwyn (1651?-87) was an actress and mistress of Charles II.

3 Louise de Kéroualle, Duchess of Portsmouth (1649-1734), a minor French aristocrat, became the leading mistress of Charles II from around 1670 until his death in 1685. She was reviled as an agent of the French and as a Catholic influence upon the king.

Appendix C: Writing for the Stage

[Writing for the stage in the early eighteenth century was a delicate task. Theatre audiences seemed to be on the wane, and the two theatre companies in London were finding it difficult to make a regular profit, even keeping to a reliable, established commercial repertoire. This, coupled with attacks on the drama and the theatre itself by social reformers and the non-juring clergyman Jeremy Collier, meant that new playwrights found writing for the stage a tricky business.]

1. Susanna Centlivre, Dedication to *The Platonick Lady* (1707)

[In her prefaces and dedications Susanna Centlivre reflected on the principles guiding her writing and the particular difficulties facing the female dramatist. Although several women playwrights including Aphra Behn, Delarivier Manley, Mary Pix, and Catharine Trotter had forged, and were forging, successful theatrical careers alongside Centlivre, there was still some prejudice against women's writing.]

To all the Generous Encouragers of Female Ingenuity, this Play is Humbly Dedicated.

Gentlemen and Ladies;

My Muse chose to make this Universal Address, hoping, among the numerous Crowd, to find some Souls Great enough to protect her against the Carping Malice of the Vulgar World; who think it proof of their Sense, to dislike every thing that is writ by Women. I was the more induc'd to this General Application, from the Usage I have met on all sides.

A Play secretly introduc'd to the House, whilst the Author remains unknown, is approv'd by every Body: The Actors cry it up, and are in expectation of a great Run; the Bookseller of a Second

Edition, and the Scribler of a Sixth Night: But if by chance the Plot's discover'd, and the Brat found Fatherless, immediately it flags in the Opinion of those that extoll'd it before, and the Bookseller falls in his Price, with this Reason only, *It is a Woman's.* Thus they alter their Judgment, by the Esteem they have for the Author, tho' the Play is still the same. They ne'er reflect, that we have had some Male-Productions of this kind, void of Plot and Wit, and full as insipid as ever a Woman's of us all.

I can't forbear inserting a Story which my Bookseller, that printed my *Gamester*, told me, of a Spark that had seen my *Gamester* three or four times, and lik'd it extremely: Having bought one of the Books, ask'd who the Author was; and being told, a Woman, threw down the book, and put up his Money, saying, he had spent too much after it already, and was sure if the Town had known that, it wou'd never have run ten days. No doubt this was a Wit in his own Eyes. It is such as these that rob us of that which inspires the Poet, Praise. And it is such as these made him that Printed my Comedy call'd, *Love's Contrivance;* or, *Medecin Malgre lui*, put two Letters of a wrong Name to it; which tho' it was the height of Injustice to me, yet his imposing on the Town turn'd to account with him; and thus passing for a Man's, it has been play'd at least a hundred times.

And why this Wrath against the Womens Works? Perhaps you'll answer, because they meddle with things out of their Sphere: But I say, no; for since the Poet is born, why not a Woman as well as a Man? Not that I wou'd derogate from those great Men who have a Genius, and Learning to improve that Genius: I only object against those ill-natur'd Criticks, who wanting both, think they have a sufficient claim to Sense, by railing at what they don't understand. Some have arm'd themselves with resolution not to like the Play they paid to see; and if in spite of Spleen they have been pleas'd against their Will, have maliciously reported it was none of mine, but given me by some Gentleman: Nay, even my own Sex, which shou'd assert our Prerogative against such Detractors, are often backward to encourage the Female Pen.

Wou'd these profest Enemies but consider what Examples we have had of Women that excell'd in all Arts; in Musick, Painting, Poetry; also in War: Nay, to our immortal Praise, what Empresses and Queens have fill'd the World? What cannot *England* boast from Women? The mighty *Romans* felt the Power of *Boadicea's* Arm; *Eliza* made *Spain* tremble; but *ANN*, the greatest of the Three, has shook the Man that aim'd at Universal Sway.[1] After naming this Miracle, the Glory of our Sex, sure none will spitefully cavil at the following Scenes, purely because a Woman writ 'em. This I dare venture to say in their behalf, there is a Plot and Story in them, I hope will entertain the Reader.

2. Susanna Centlivre, Preface to *Love's Contrivance* (1703)

THE PREFACE

Writing is a kind of Lottery in this fickle Age, and Dependence on the Stage as precarious as the Cast of a Die; the Chance may turn up, and a Man may write to please the Town, but 'tis uncertain, since we see our best Authors sometimes fail. The Criticks cavil most about Decorums, and crie up *Aristotle's* Rules[2] as the most essential part of the Play; I own they are in the right of it, yet I dare venture a Wager they'll never persuade the Town to be of their Opinion, which relishes nothing so well as Humour lightly tost up with Wit, and drest with Modesty and Air. And I believe Mr. *Rich*[3] will own, he got more by the *Trip to the Jubilee*,[4] with all its Irregularities, than by the most uniform Piece the Stage cou'd boast of e'er since. I do not say this by way of condemning the Unity of Time, Place, and Action; quite contrary, for I think them the greatest Beauties of a Dramatick Poem; but since the other way of writing pleases full as well, and gives the Poet a larger Scope of Fancy, and with less Trouble, Care, and Pains, serves his and

---

1 Louis XIV, in Queen Anne and the Whig party's prosecution of the War of the Spanish Succession.

2 French neoclassical dramatists and critics, and English dramatists and poets of the late seventeenth century, embellished an idealised notion of the unity of action in tragedy that Aristotle had expounded in his *Poetics*, and evolved prescriptive rules requiring drama to display the unities of action (one main plotline), place (one physical place represented), and time (events to take place over no more that twenty-four hours).

3 Christopher Rich, manager of the patent company at Drury Lane Theatre.

4 George Farquhar's *The Constant Couple; or, A Trip to the Jubilee* (1699) was a Drury Lane success which reputedly had as many as fifty-three performances in its first season.

the Players End, why shou'd a Man torture, and wrack his Brain for what will be no Advantage to him. This I dare engage, that the Town will ne'er be entertain'd with Plays according to the Method of the Ancients, till they exclude this Innovation of Wit and Humour, which yet I see no likelihood of doing. The following Poem I think has nothing can disoblige the nicest Ear; and tho' I did not observe the Rules of *Drama*, I took peculiar Care to dress my Thoughts in such a modest Stile, that it might not give Offence to any. Some Scenes I confess are partly taken from *Molier* [*sic*], and I dare be bold to say it has not suffer'd in the Translation: I thought 'em pretty in the French, and cou'd not help believing they might divert in an English Dress. The French have that light Airiness in their Temper, that the least Glimps [*sic*] of Wit sets them a laughing, when 'twould not make us so much as smile; so that where I found the Stile too poor, I endeavour'd to give it a Turn; for who e'er borrows from them, must take care to touch the Colours with an English Pencil, and form the Piece according to our Manners. When first I took those Scenes of *Molier*'s, I design'd but three Acts; for that reason I chose such as suited best with Farce, which indeed are all that sort you'll find in it; for what I added to 'em, I believe the Reader will allow to be a different Stile, at least some very good Judges thought so, and in spight of me divided it into five Acts, believing it might pass amongst the Comedies of these Times. And indeed I have no reason to complain, for I confess it met a Reception beyond my Expectation: I must own my self infinitely oblig'd to the Players, and in a great Measure the Success was owing to them, especially Mr. *Wilks*,[1] who extended his Faculties to such a Pitch, that one may almost say he out-play'd himself; and the Town must confess they never saw three different Characters by one Man acted so well before, and I think my self extremely indebted to him, likewise to Mr. *Johnson*,[2] who in his way I think the best Comedian of the Age.

---

1   Robert Wilks (ca.1665-1732), leading actor, and later actor-manager, at Drury Lane.
2   Benjamin Johnson (ca.1665-1742), scene-painter and actor at Drury Lane.

3. From Jeremy Collier, *A Short View of the Immorality and Profaneness of the English Stage* (1698): A2-4, 1-2, 6-8, 285-88

[Jeremy Collier (1650-1726) was a non-juring Anglican clergyman, pamphleteer, and social reformer. This tract began a long battle between theatre personnel and the social reformers of the day over the legitimacy of the stage. Centlivre's *The Basset Table* was hailed by some as an example of the kind of reformed drama emerging in response to Collier's outburst.]

The Preface
Being convinc'd that nothing has gone farther in Debauching the Age than the Stage Poets, and Play-House, I thought I could not employ my time better than in writing against them. These Men sure, take Vertue and Regularity, for great Enemies, why else is their Disaffection so very Remarkable?

It must be said, They have made their Attack with great Courage, and gain'd no inconsiderable Advantage. But it seems Lewdness without Atheism, is but half their Business. Conscience might possibly recover, and Revenge be thought on; and therefore like Foot-Pads, they must not only Rob, but Murther. To do them right their Measures are Politickly taken: To make sure work on't, there's nothing like Destroying of Principles; Practise must follow of Course. For to have no good Principles, is to have no Reason to be Good. Now 'tis not to be expected that people should check their Appetites, and balk their Satisfactions, they don't know why. If Vertue has no Prospect, 'tis not worth the owning. Who would be troubled with Conscience if 'tis only a Bugbear, and has nothing in't but Vision and the Spleen.

My collection from the English Stage, is much short of what They are able to furnish. An Inventory of their Ware-House would have been a large Work: But being afraid of over charging the Reader, I thought a Pattern might do.

...

The Introduction
The business of Plays is to recommend Vertue, and discountenance Vice; To shew the Uncertainty of Humane Greatness, the suddain

Turns of Fate, and the Unhappy Conclusions of Violence and Injustice: 'Tis to expose the Singularities of Pride and Fancy, to make Folly and Falsehood contemptible, and to bring every Thing that is Ill under Infamy, and Neglect. This Design has been oddly pursued by the English Stage. Our Poets write with a different View, and are gone into an other Interest. 'Tis true, were their Intentions fair, they might be Serviceable to this Purpose. They have in a great measure the Springs of Thought and Inclination in their Power. Show, Musick, Action, and Rhetorick are moving Entertainments; and rightly employ'd would be very significant. But Force and Motion are Things indifferent, and the Use lies chiefly in the Application. These Advantages are now, in the Enemies Hand, and under a very dangerous Management. Like Canon seized they are pointed the wrong way, and by the Strength of the Defence the Mischief is made the greater. That this Complaint is not unreasonable I shall endeavour to prove by shewing the Misbehaviour of the Stage with respect to Morality and Religion. Their Liberties in the Following Particulars are intolerable. Their Smuttiness of Expression; Their Swearing, Profainness, and Lewd Application of Scripture; Their Abuse of the Clergy; Their making their Top Characters Libertines, and giving them Success in their Debauchery. This Charge, with some other Irregularities, I shall make good against the Stage, and shew both the Novelty and Scandal of the Practise.

...

The Immodesty of the Stage
Smuttiness is a Fault in Behaviour as well as in Religion. 'Tis a very Coarse Diversion, the Entertainment of those who are generally least both in Sense, and Station. The looser part of the Mob, have no true relish of Decency and Honour, and want Education, and Thought, to furnish out a gentile Conversation. Barrenness of Fancy makes them often take up with those Scandalous Liberties. A Vitious Imagination may blot a great deal of Paper at this rate with ease enough: And 'tis possible Convenience may sometimes invite to the Expedient. The Modern Poets seem to use Smut as the Old Ones did Machines, to relieve a fainting Invention. When

Pegasus is jaded,[1] and would stand still, he is apt like other Tits, to run into every Puddle.

Obscenity in any Company is a rustick uncreditable Talent; but among Women 'tis particularly rude. Such Talk would be very affrontive in Conversation, and not endur'd by any Lady of Reputation. Whence then comes it to Pass that those Liberties which disoblige so much in Conversation, should entertain upon the Stage. Do the Women leave all the regards to Decency and Conscience behind them when they come to the Play-House? Or does the Place transform their Inclinations, and turn their former Aversion into Pleasure? Or were Their pretences to Sobriety elsewhere nothing but Hypocrisy and Grimace? Such Suppositions as these are all Satyr and Invective: They are rude Imputations upon the whole Sex. To treat the Ladys with such stuff is no better than taking their Money to abuse them. It supposes their Imagination vitious, and their Memories ill furnish'd: That they are practised in the Languages of the Stews, and pleas'd with the Scenes of Brutishness. When at the same time the Customs of Education, and the Laws of Decency, are so very cautious, and reserv'd in regard to Women: I say so very reserv'd, that 'tis almost a Fault for them to Understand they are ill Used.

They can't discover their Disgust without disadvantage, nor Blush without disservice to their Modesty. To appear with any skill in such Cant, looks as if they had fallen upon ill Conversation; or Managed their Curiosity amiss. In a word, He that treats the Ladys with such Discourse, must conclude either that they like it, or they do not. To suppose the first, is a gross Reflection upon their Virtue. And as for the latter case, it entertains them with their own Aversion; which is ill Nature and ill Manners enough in all Conscience. And in this Particular, Custom and Conscience, the Forms of Breeding, and the Maxims of Religion are on the same side.

...

1 Pegasus, a winged horse of Greek mythology, was often represented as carrying the Muses or poets on flights of creative imagination. A jade was slang for a worn-out horse, and was frequently used metaphorically to represent the faltering rhyme or inspiration of poets; see Alexander Pope's *An Essay on Criticism* (1709).

And here I can't imagine how we can reconcile such Liberties with our Profession. These Entertainments are as it were Litterally renounc'd in Baptism. They are the *Vanities of the wicked World, and the Works of the Devil*,[1] in the most open, and emphatical Signification. *What Communion has Light with Darkness, and what concord has Christ with Belial*.[2] Call you this Diversion? Can Profaness be such an irresistible Delight? Does the Crime of the Performance make the Spirit of the Satisfaction, and is the Scorn of Christianity the Entertainment of Christians? Is it such a Pleasure to hear the Scriptures burlesqu'd? Is Ribaldry so very obliging, and Atheism so Charming a Quality? Are we indeed willing to quit the Privilege of our Nature; to surrender our Charter of Immortality, and throw up the Pretences to another Life? It may be so! But then we should do well to remember that Nothing is not in our Power. Our Desires did not make us, neither can they unmake us. But I hope our wishes are not so mean, and that we have a better sense of the Dignity of our Being. And if so, how can we be pleas'd with those Things which would degrade us into Brutes, which ridicule our Creed, and turn all our Expectations into Romance.

And after all, the Jest on't is, these Men would make us believe their design is Virtue and Reformation. In good time! They are likely to combat Vice with success who destroy the Principles of Good and Evil! Take them at the best, and they do no more than expose a little Humour, and Formality. But then, as the Matter is manag'd, the Correction is much worse than the Fault. They laugh at Pedantry, and teach Atheism, cure a Pimple and give the Plague. I heartily wish they would have let us alone. To exchange Virtue for Behaviour is a hard Bargain. Is not plain Honesty much better than Hypocrisy well Dress'd? What's Sight good for without Substance? What is a well bred Libertine but a well bred Knave? One that can't prefer Conscience to Pleasure, without calling himself Fool: And will sell his Friend, or his Father, if need be, for his Convenience.

In short: Nothing can be more disserviceable to Probity and Religion, than the management of the Stage. It cherishes those

---

1 This phrase echoes the baptismal catechism of the Church of England, laid out in *The Book of Common Prayer*.

2 This is a phrase from 2 *Corinthians* 6, verses 14 & 15.

Passions, and rewards those Vices, which 'tis the business of Reason to discountenance. It strikes at the Root of Principle, draws off the Inclinations from Virtue, and spoils good Education: 'Tis the most effectual means to baffle the Force of Discipline, to emasculate peoples Spirits, and Debauch their Manners. How many of the Unwary have these Syrens devour'd? And how often has the best Blood been tainted, with this Infection? What Disappointment of Parents, what Confusion in Families, and What Beggery in Estates have been hence occasion'd? And which is still worse, the Mischief spreads dayly, and the Malignity grows more envenom'd.

The Feavour works up towards Madness and will scarcely endure to be touch'd. And what hope is there of Health when the Patient strikes in with the Disease, and flies in the Face of the Remedy? Can Religion retrive us? Yes, when we don't despise it. But while our Notions are naught, our Lives will hardly be otherwise. What can the Assistance of the Church signify to those who are more ready to Rally the Preacher, than Practice the Sermon? To those who are overgrown with Pleasure, and hardned in Ill Custom? Who have neither Patience to hear, nor Conscience to take hold of? You may almost as well feed a Man without a Mouth, as give Advice where there's no disposition to receive it.... For this miserable Temper, we may thank the Stage in great Measure: And therefore, if I mistake not, They have the least pretence to Favour, and the most need of Repentance, of all Men Living.

4. From John Dennis, *The Usefulness of the Stage* (1698): Introduction, 23-26

[John Dennis (1657-1734), critic, poet, and author of several plays, was one of the first and most fulsome respondents to Collier. As Dennis articulates here, some theatre personnel saw Collier's attack as an attempt not to reform the drama, but to close the theatres.]

Introduction
The best things here below are liable to be corrupted, and the better things are in their own natures, the more mischievous are they if corrupted. For that which is superlatively good in it self

can be corrupted by nothing but extraordinary malice. Since then the Stage is acknowledg'd by its greatest adversaries to be in itself good, and instrumental to the instruction of mankind, nothing can be more unreasonable than to exhort people to ruin it instead of reforming it, since at that rate we must think of abolishing much more important establishments. Yet that is apparently the design of Mr Collier's Book, tho his malice infinitely surpassing his ability, as it certainly does, whatever some people may think of him, his performance is some what awkward. For in the Introduction to his Book he gives you reasons why the Stage in general ought to be commended; in the first Chapters of his Book he pretends to shew cause why the English Stage ought to be reform'd and in the sixth and last Chapter, he pretends to prove by Authority that no Stage ought to be allow'd. In the beginning of his Book he produces his own reasons why the Stage reform'd ought to be encourag'd, and in the end of the same Book he brings other mens opinions to shew that every Stage ought to be abolish'd; and so endeavours to ruine his own Reasons by a long scroll of other peoples Authorities, which is certainly a pleasant condescension; but such is the fantastick humility of pedantick pride....

If Mr Collier had only attack'd the Corruptions of the Stage, for my own part I should have been so far from blaming him, that I should have publickly return'd him my thanks: For the abuses are so great, that there is necessity for the reforming them; not that I think that with all its corruptions the Stage has debauch'd the people: I am fully convinc'd it has not, and I believe I have said enough in the following treatise to convince the Reader of it. But this is certain, that the corruptions of the Stage hinder its efficacy in the reformation of manners. For, besides that Vice is contrary to Virtue, it renders the Stage little and contemptible; for nothing but Virtue can make anything awful and truly great, and nothing but what is awful and truly great can be universally respected, and by that means in a condition to influence the minds of the people. For this reason, as I said above, if Mr Collier had only attack'd the licentiousness of the Stage, in so fair a manner as he ought to have done it, I had return'd him my thanks, but when I found by this last Chapter, that his design was against the Stage itself I thought I could not spend a month more usefully; than in the vindication of it....

The method that I have used has been this: I have endeavour'd to shew that the Stage in general is useful to the happiness of Mankind, to the welfare of Government and the advancement of Religion; And under the head of Government I have endeavour'd to prove, that the Stage does not encourage Revenge, as Mr Collier asserts in his last Chapter; and that by encouraging Pride, which is another thing that he charges upon it, it provides for the happiness of particular men, and the publick. I have endeavour'd to shew too, in the defence of the English Stage, that it is to be commended for its impartiality, and in exempting no degree or order of men from censure.

...

That the Corruption of Manners is not to be attributed to the licentiousness of the Drama, may appear from the consideration of the reigning vices, I mean those moral vices which have more immediate influence upon mens conduct, and consequently upon their happiness. And those are chiefly four.

    1. The love of Women.

    2. Drinking.

    3. Gaming.

    4. Unnatural sins.

For drinking and gaming, their excesses cannot be reasonably charg'd upon the Stage, for the following Reasons.

First, Because it cannot possibly be conceiv'd, that so reasonable a Diversion as the Drama, can encourage or incline men to so unreasonable a one as gaming, or so brutal a one as drunkenness.

Secondly, Because these two vices have been made odious and ridiculous by our Plays, instead of being shewn agreeable. As for Drunkenness, to shew the sinner is sufficient to discredit the vice; for a Drunkard of necessity always appears either odious or ridiculous. And for a Gamester, I never knew any one shewn in a Play, but either as a Fool or a Rascal.

Thirdly, Because those two vices flourish in places that are too remote, and in persons that are too abject to be encourag'd or influenc'd by the Stage. There is drinking and gaming in the furthest North and the furthest West, among Peasants, as well as among Dukes and Peers. But here perhaps some vision-ary Zealot will urge, that these two vices, even these remote places, and these abject persons proceed from the influence of that irreligion, which is caus'd by the corruptions of the Stage, and will with as much reason as modesty deduce the lewdness which is transacted in the Tin mines, in Cornwall, and in the Coal-pits of Newcastle, from the daily abominations of the Pits of the two Playhouses, as he would derive the brutality of the high Dutch Drinking, from the prophaneness of our English Drama.

But what will he say then to those Gentlemen, who neither are suppos'd to go to our Theatres, nor to converse much with those who do, nor to be liable to be corrupted by them; what will they say to these Gentlemen, if they can be prov'd to have a considerable share of the two fore-mention'd vices? What can they answer? For it would be ridiculously absurd to reply, that the Clergy are cor-rupted by the Laity, whom it is their business to convert. But here I think my self oblig'd to declare, that I by no means design this as a reflection upon the Church of England, who I am satisfy'd may more justly boast of its Clergy, than any other Church whatsoever; a Clergy that are equally illustrious for their Piety and for their Learning, yet may I venture to affirm, that there are some among them, who can never be suppos'd to have been corrupted by Play-houses, who yet turn up a Bottle oftner than they do an Hour-glass, who box about a pair of Tables with more fervour than they do their Cushions, contemplate a pair of Dice more frequently than the Fathers or Councels, and meditate and depend upon Hazard, more than they do upon Providence.

5. From Colley Cibber, *The Lady's Last Stake* (1707): Dedication

[Colley Cibber (1671-1757), actor, manager, and playwright, was always quick to spot a rising trend. He followed the fashion for gaming plays with this offering, which he claimed would meet the demands of the social reformers, and hoped would gratify the most genteel audience members.]

To the Most Noble The Marquis of Kent, Lord Chamberlain of Her Majesty's Houshold, &c.

The utmost Success I ever propos'd from this Play, was, that it might reach the Taste of a few good Judges, and from thence plead a sort of Title to your Lordship's Protection: And if the most just and candid Criticks are not the greatest Flatterers, I have not fail'd in my Proposal. As for those Gentlemen that thrust themselves forward upon the Stage before a crowded Audience, as if they resolv'd to play themselves, and save the Actor the trouble of presenting them, they indeed, as they are above Instruction, so they scorn to be diverted by it, and will as soon allow me a good Voice as a Genius. I did not intend it shou'd entertain any, that never come with a Design to sit out a Play; and therefore, without being much mortified, am content such Persons shou'd dislike it. If I would have been less instructive, I might easily have had a louder, tho' not a more valuable Applause. But I shall always prefer a fixt and general Attention before the noisy Roars of the Gallery. A Play, without a just Moral, is a poor and mercenary Undertaking; and 'tis from the Success of such Pieces, that Mr. Collier was furnish'd with an Advantageous Pretence of laying his unmerciful Axe to the Root of the Stage. Gaming is a Vice, that has undone more innocent Principles, than any one Folly that's in Fashion, therefore I chose to expose it to the Fair Sex in its most hideous Form, by reducing a Woman of Honour to stand the presuming Adresses of a Man, whom neither her Vertue or Inclination wou'd let her have the least Taste to: Now 'tis not impossible but some Man of Fortune, who has a handsome Lady, and a great deal of Money to throw away, may from this startling hint think it worth his while to find his Wife some less hazardous Diversion. If that should ever happen, my End of writing this Play is answer'd; and if it may boast of any Favours from the Town, I now must own they are entirely owing to your Lordship's Protection of the Theatre. For, without a Union of the best Actors, it must have been impossible for it to have receiv'd a tolerable Justice in the Performance.

Appendix D: Criticism of Centlivre and The Basset Table

[Theatre reviewing had not yet established itself in the early eighteenth century. Commentary on the drama of the day emerges in other forms of periodical, pamphlet, or essay writing. *The Basset Table* aroused very little commentary at the time, except in Arthur Bedford's anti-theatrical polemic. One of the first literary assessments of Centlivre's dramatic writing comes much later from Richard Cumberland's early nineteenth-century *The British Drama*.]

1. From Arthur Bedford, *The Evil and Danger of Stage Plays* (Bristol, 1706): 127–29

[Arthur Bedford (1668–1745) was a Bristol clergyman who took up the message of Jeremy Collier's *A Short View of the Immorality and Profaneness of the English Stage* (1698) and pursued his own vendetta against the stage. He was the first to comment on Centlivre's *Basset Table*. Although in her dedication Centlivre paid lip-service to the idea that the play was intended to "rectify Manners," Bedford remained unconvinced.]

But some object, Are there not later *Plays* written, to expose the vices of the Age, particularly the *Gamester* and the *Basset Table*? and will not such contribute very much towards a *Reformation*?

To this I answer, That the chief Matter, which the *Plays* Expose, is a little *Pedantry, Humour* and *Formality*, a Country Clown, or an affected *Gate*, which signifies nothing in Matters of *Religion*, and is in no respect inconsistent with the *Civil Government*. It may also be granted, that they sometimes expose *Covetousness*, being a *Vice* directly against their Interest, and consequently as odious to them as *Religion* and *Reformation*. But to expose *Covetousness*, before a Company of *Rakes, Spendthrifts,* and *Prodigals* (for such are most of those who resort to the *Play-Houses*) serves rather to sooth them in their *Vices*, and harden them in the contrary *Sin*. The *Gamester*, and the *Basset Table*, are written by the same Author, and (omitting several exceptionable Passages), are very little serviceable to the pretended Design. The Epilogue of the *Gamester*, speaks against this particular *Vice*; but the Design of the *Play*, and the Conduct of *Valere* the *Gamester* seems rather to infer, that *It is good to have Two Strings to our Bow*. If we Game and succeed therein we are provided for; if that fails we shall pass for Gentlemen, and may marry rich Fortunes; and tho' we break our *Oaths* and *Promises* which we made at first, yet the Ladies will soon believe us at another Time. For my Part I expect no good from a *Play* were [*sic*] the *Devil* is invok'd in the very first Line, and believe our *Reformation* must be carried on without his Assistance. However, the Author seems sensible that there might be good *Morality* in the *Epilogue* of the *Gamester*, and therefore takes Care to be guilty of no such Fault in the *Epilogue* of *The Basset Table*; and as in the other *Valere* was a Loser, so in this *The Lady Reveller* games and wins, and is afterward married to the *Lord Worthy*, one of the best *Reputation*. In short, in these two *Plays* are contained all, I think, that they can boast of in two Years, which serves to reform a *Vice* to which their *Hearers* may be inclin'd. From these their Champions make the great Noise of their *Reformation*, and these serve rather to amuse the World, than to amend it.

2. From Richard Cumberland, "Critique," *The British Drama* (London, 1817), vol. 7

[Richard Cumberland (1732–1811), playwright and critic, included Centlivre's *The Busie Body, The Wonder*, and *A Bold Stroke for a Wife* in his fourteen volume collection of the best of British theatre, indicating Centlivre's enduring popularity. This comment on Centlivre's style of writing prefaced her play, *The Busie Body*.]

Mrs. Centlivre, after the taste of Mrs. Aphra Behn, was a writer of that Comedy, which may be termed the *Intriguing* Drama—built upon chance medley and situation, mistakes, closets, veils, balconies, old guardians, and young profligates, with a set of ladies who seem bound by no other laws than their inclinations.

I know, positively, no one of her plays which, morally speaking, may not do mischief; but they have bustle, they have business, and carrying the commercial passion with them into their amusements, the English love that their drama should be crowded with *character*, and that its personages should be all people in *plentiful business*.

What may, when her outset in life is considered, be deemed surprising, is, that her comedies all evidence very forcibly for her acquirements in learning;—her assiduity must have augmented with her years,

"Vires acquirit eundo."[1]

For the modern languages were obviously her own; and of Latin she seems to have had more than to females is usually given, even where the education has been regular.

She was assuredly an illustrious female author—But the literary Ladies of our *own times* dim all preceding claims to the rank of Dramatic Writers—Mrs. Cowley,[2] Miss Lee,[3] and the Novel Dramatist Burney.[4]

---

1   Roughly translates as "she gathers strength as she goes," a frequently used motto from Virgil's *Aeneid*; see Book IV, line 175.

2   Hannah Cowley (1743-1809) was a poet and playwright, whose theatrical career started when Garrick staged *The Runaway* (1776). Cowley's two best known comedies are *The Belle's Stratagem* (1780) and *A Bold Stroke for a Husband* (1783).

3   Sophia Lee (ca. 1750-1824) was a novelist and playwright from a theatrical family. Her comedies, *The Chapter of Accidents* (1780), *The Assignation* (1807), and her tragedy, *Almeyda* (1796), were extremely successful.

4   Frances Burney (1752-1840) was better known as a novelist in her own day. The only play to be staged during her lifetime, the tragedy *Edwy and Elgiva* (1795), lasted one night. Her comedies, including *A Busy Day* (ca. 1802) and satiric *The Witlings* (ca. 1778), and her other tragedies, have received more attention from recent scholars.

Works Cited

Anderson, Misty. *Female Playwrights and Eighteenth-Century Comedy: Negotiating Marriage on the London Stage*. New York: Palgrave, 2002.

Astell, Mary. *A Serious Proposal to the Ladies ... In Two Parts*. London, 1697.

Bedford, Arthur. *The Evil and Danger of Stage Plays*. Bristol, 1706.

Berry, Helen. "An Early Coffee House Periodical and its Readers: *The Athenian Mercury*, 1691-1697." *The London Journal* 25.1 (2000): 14-33.

Bowyer, John. *The Celebrated Mrs Centlivre*. Durham, NC: Duke UP, 1952.

Boyer, Abel. *Letters of Wit, Politicks and Morality*. London, 1701.

Bratton, Jacky. "Reading the Intertheatrical; or, The Mysterious Disappearance of Susanna Centlivre." *Women, Theatre and Performance: New Histories, New Historiographies*. Ed. Maggie Gale and Viv Gardner. Manchester: Manchester UP, 2000.

Copeland, Nancy. *Staging Gender in Behn and Centlivre*. Aldershot: Ashgate, 2004.

Defoe, Daniel. *An Anatomy of Exchange Alley*. London, 1719.

——— . *An Essay upon Projects*. London, 1697.

Descartes, René. "Letters to Henry More," *The Philosophical Writings of Descartes*. Trans. J. Cottingham, R. Stoothoff, D. Murdoch, and A. Kenny. Cambridge: Cambridge UP, 1991.

Egerton, William. *Faithful Memoirs of the Life, Amours and Performances of ... Mrs. Anne Oldfield*. London, 1731.

Evans, James E. "'A Sceane of Uttmost Vanity': The Spectacle of Gambling in Late Stuart Culture." *Studies in Eighteenth-Century Culture* 31 (2002): 1-20.

——— . "Libertine Gamblers in Late Stuart Comedy." *Restoration and Eighteenth-Century Theatre Research* 18.1 (2003): 17-30.

Fontenelle, Bernard de. *A Discovery of New Worlds*. Trans. Aphra Behn. London, 1688.

Frushell, Richard. "Biographical Problems and Satisfactions in Susanna Centlivre." *Restoration and Eighteenth-Century Theatre Research* 7.2 (1992): 16-38.

———, ed. *The Plays of Susanna Centlivre*. New York: Garland, 1982.

Henry, John. *The Scientific Revolution and the Origins of Modern Science*. Basingstoke: Macmillan, 1997.

Herrell, LuAnn Venden. "'Luck Be a Lady Tonight,' or at Least Make Me a Gentleman: Economic Anxiety in Centlivre's *The Gamester*." *Studies in the Literary Imagination* 32. 2 (1999): 45-61.

Hume, Robert D. *The Development of English Drama in the Late Seventeenth Century*. Oxford: Clarendon, 1976.

Jacob, Giles. *The Poetical Register: or, The Lives and Characters of the English Dramatick Poets*. London, 1719.

Jardine, Lisa. *Ingenious Pursuits: Building the Scientific Revolution*. London: Little, Brown and Co., 1999.

Kavanagh, Thomas. *Enlightenment and the Shadows of Chance: The Novel and the Culture of Gambling in Eighteenth-Century France*. Baltimore: Johns Hopkins UP, 1993.

Kreis-Schinck, Annette. *Women, Writing, and the Theater in the Early Modern Period: the Plays of Aphra Behn and Suzanne Centlivre*. Madison, NJ: Fairleigh Dickinson UP, 2001.

Levin, Kate. "*The Basset Table* in Performance." *Restoration and Eighteenth-Century Theatre Research* 16 (2001): 97-111.

Lock, F.P. *Susanna Centlivre*. Boston: Twayne-G.K. Hall, 1979.

Lucas, Theophilus. *Memoirs of the Lives, Intrigues, and Comical Adventures of the most Famous Gamesters*. London, 1714.

Milhous, Judith and Robert Hume, eds. *Roscius Anglicanus*. London: Society for Theatre Research, 1987.

———. "Playwrights' Remuneration in Eighteenth-Century London." *Huntington Library Quarterly* 10.2-3 (1999): 3-90.

Mottley, John (?). "A Compleat List of All the English Dramatic Poets." Appended to Thomas Whincop, *Scanderbeg*. London, 1747.

Pearson, Jacqueline. *The Prostituted Muse: Images of Women and Women Dramatists 1642-1737*. New York: St Martin's, 1988.

———, ed. *Susanna Centlivre*. vol. 3 *Eighteenth-Century Women Playwrights*. Gen. ed. Derek Hughes. London: Pickering and Chatto, 2001.

———. "Textual Variants and Inconsistencies in Susanna Centlivre's *The Basset-Table* (1705)." *Restoration and Eighteenth-Century Theatre Research* 15.2 (2000): 40-59.

Pepys, Samuel. *The Diary of Samuel Pepys.* Ed. Robert Latham and William Matthews. 10 vols. Berkeley: U of California P, 1974.

Rigamonti, Antonella and Laura Favero Carraro. "Women at Stake: The Self-Assertive Potential of Gambling in Susanna Centlivre's *The Basset Table.*" *Restoration and Eighteenth-Century Theatre Research* 16.2 (2001): 53–62.

Rosenthal, Laura. *Playwrights and Plagiarists in Early Modern England: Gender, Authorship and Literary Property.* Ithaca: Cornell UP, 1996.

Savile, George. "Advice to a Daughter." *Miscellanies by the late Marquis of Halifax.* London, 1704.

Shank, J.B. "Neither Natural Philosophy, Nor Science, Nor Literature." *Men, Women and the Birthing of Modern Science.* Ed. Judith Zinsser. DeKalb: Northern Illinois UP, 2005.

Southerne, Thomas. *A Maid's Last Prayer.* London, 1693.

Sprat, Thomas. *History of the Royal* Society. London, 1702.

Staves, Susan. "Investments, Votes and Bribes: Women as Shareholders in the Chartered National Companies." *Women Writers and the Early Modern British Political Tradition.* Ed. Hilda Smith. Cambridge: Cambridge UP, 1998.

Stewart, Larry. *The Rise of Public Science.* Cambridge: Cambridge UP, 1992.

Sutherland, James R. "The Progress of Error: Mrs. Centlivre and the Biographers." *Review of English Studies* 18.72 (1942): 167–82.

Van Leeuwenhoek, Anthony. "An Extract of a Letter from Mr. Anthony Van Leeuwenhoek, to the R.S. Containing His Observations on ... the Skin of the Hand, and Pores, of Sweat, the Crystalline Humour, Optic Nerves, Gall, and Scales of Fish." *Philosophical Transactions (1683-1775)* 17 (1693): 949–60.

van Lennep, William, Emmet L. Avery, et al., eds. *The London Stage 1660-1800.* Carbondale: Southern Illinois UP, 1960-68.

Wallace, Beth Kowalski. "A Modest Defence of Gaming Women." *Studies in Eighteenth-Century Culture* 31 (2002): 21–40.

Warren, Victoria. "Gender and Genre in Susanna Centlivre's *The Gamester* and *The Basset Table.*" *Studies in English Literature, 1500-1900* 43.3 (2003): 605–24.

From the Publisher

A name never says it all, but the word "Broadview" expresses a good deal of the philosophy behind our company. We are open to a broad range of academic approaches and political viewpoints. We pay attention to the broad impact book publishing and book printing has in the wider world; for some years now we have used 100% recycled paper for most titles. Our publishing program is internationally oriented and broad-ranging. Our individual titles often appeal to a broad reader-ship too; many are of interest as much to general readers as to academics and students.

Founded in 1985, Broadview remains a fully independent company owned by its shareholders—not an imprint or subsidiary of a larger multinational.

For the most accurate information on our books (including information on pricing, editions, and formats) please visit our website at www.broadviewpress.com. Our print books and ebooks are also available for sale on our site.

broadview press
www.broadviewpress.com